This book is a memoir. It depicts actual events in my life as truthfully as recollection permits. In it feels important to say, I am but one participant. I have done my best to offer my most generous interpretation of all other viewpoints, and if others want to write their own book, I say I can't wait to read it. All persons within are actual individuals; there are no composite characters but the names of some individuals have been changed because they have either been denied a measure of respect by professionals, and I don't trust them.

Paperback ISBN 979-8-9903249-0-9

First publication 2024

Thank You for Failing Me

Stephanie Smith Skipper

Thank You for Failing Me

Stephanie Smith Skipper

SOHO

Dad, this book is for you.

I wish I knew more of you.

And...

It is my honor to share what I do know with the world.

You have always been worth knowing.

I love you.

TABLE OF CONTENTS

Content Warning and Mental Health Resources

Chapter 1: A Slip of The Tongue, A Broken Heart

Chapter 2: Pain Reveals Passion

Chapter 3: We All Come from Somewhere

Chapter 4: My Dad Broke Up with Me

Chapter 5: Chasing the Dream

Chapter 6: A Hero or Zero?

Chapter 7: Marriage

Chapter 8: A Fist Fight with Reality

Chapter 9: Put Your Hand on Your "Knower"

Chapter 10: Joining A Club No One Wants to Be Part Of

Chapter 11: Who Knew I Really Sucked at Boundaries

Chapter 12: Coconut Coffee

Chapter 13: Taking Responsibility

Chapter 14: Happy Birthday Dad

Chapter 15: An 8-Hour Drive for Breakfast

Chapter 16: The Visit

Chapter 17: The Phone Call

Chapter 18: Communal Mourning

Epilogue: Where We Are Now

A Benediction

About the Author

Content Warning

This book contains themes of abandonment, addiction, depression, and suicide. While the content of this book is meant to be hopeful, both to those who suffer from mental illness and to those who love someone with a mental illness, some presented themes may be difficult for some readers.

Mental Health is Something to Take Seriously

Since the age of 14, psychological therapy has been a part of my life in varying degrees and will be something I continue to practice. In addition, throughout two particularly difficult seasons of my mental health journey, I found myself in need of medication to help my recovery. Despite my momentary fear and shame over needing extra help, I found the meds to be beneficial, and I am grateful they were available to me.

The best way I've heard the healthy use of medication described was by Al Andrews at Porter's Call. He saw my exhaustion from treading water, desperately trying to stay afloat in my life, and asked me if I would reach for a life jacket if it were available.

"You'd still have to do the work of swimming to shore; the medication doesn't fix everything," he said, "But you wouldn't be burning all your energy trying to stay afloat. Instead, you could use it to get to steady land."

If you feel like you're treading water, the thought of swimming to shore may sound impossible. You may become discouraged by how far you've drifted from land, perhaps even forgetting what it's like to have stable ground beneath you. Naturally, giving up feels like an appealing option. But what if a life jacket is available to you?

If you are struggling with your mental health, my hope is you will dare to believe there is help available to you; that you are worth fighting for, and people deeply care about your well-being. I know the phone might feel like it's 700 pounds and 100 miles away. I know it takes courage and energy to pick it up. But one call (or text) can be the first step towards healing.

Here are some resources – life jackets - that are always available to you, no matter where you are. If you find yourself in need of them, please reach for them.

- The National Suicide Prevention Lifeline: 1-800-273-8255
- **Crisis Text Line**: (text HELLO to 741741)
- American Foundation for Suicide Prevention: **www.afsp.org**
- The **Veterans Crisis Line**: Dial 1-800-273-8255 and Press 1 to talk to someone or send a text message to 838255 to connect with a VA responder.
- **Better Help**: www.betterhelp.com

Chapter 1
A Slip of The Tongue, A Broken Heart

I think he might be here. A dull electricity fluttered down my arms at the thought; I had longed for this encounter for 14 years.

My brother Matt, typically an early riser and punctual, was dragging his feet in the hotel room, as Mommy kept threatening that we were going to be late. I, on the other hand, was drawn to the door, anxious to face possibility. My imagination brimmed as I fantasized about how our first conversation might go if he was there—no, he would be there.

I had never met him, but I felt I had so much in common with him. Sitting on the bed in the stuffy hotel room, waiting for my brother to knot his tie, I could feel my mother's dilemma. Sensitive to the disparity in her ducklings, she was trying to prepare us for the unknown, while also trying to move us out the door, straight into it.

We'd arrived in Hammond, Louisiana, two days after Thanksgiving. Aunts, uncles, and cousins had gathered around my grandma Billie's dining room table in Pennsylvania. Her home was a landing place for extended family, scattered all over the country.

Sitting at her large table—complete with the extender, typically stored in the coat closet—I was home. I had lived the better part of my first two years of life under that roof. The table was familiar. Matt and I joined Grandpa and Grandma for dinner at least once a week when Mommy worked late.

I had been on cloud nine that day. I was a freshman in high school and had my very first boyfriend. He was a year older than me, in my brother's class, and was training to be an Olympic swimmer. It was all so new and exciting.

Only days before, I had gone to one of his swim meets. Sitting in the stands, watching him win first place, I delighted in the idea that this guy liked me back! After the meet, we shared a special moment together in the balcony, and he became my first *real* kiss. By that, I mean he slipped me some tongue. Now, perhaps it was because I'd seen one too many gum commercials, but in all my fantasizing about what a French kiss would be like, it never occurred to me that it would be warm. I was so taken aback by it not being like the refreshing blast of minty ice marketed to me that I locked up. He had to ask if I was okay, and I privately vowed to never tell anyone that I thought kissing with tongue was going to be anything other than approximately 98.6 degrees.

When we wrapped up Thanksgiving dinner that night, our bellies were full. Mommy, Matt, and I headed to our house, only five miles across town on October Drive. The blinking red light of the answering machine immediately caught our attention as we walked into our dark house. It held a message that changed my life forever.

My great grandmother - my dad's grandmother – had passed, and we would be heading to Louisiana. Because cell phones weren't a thing yet, my mom frequented pay phones in the airport to connect with her estranged former in-laws as we traveled from Central Pennsylvania. She was attempting to gather information on whether her ex-husband, my father, would be attending or not.

No one could give us an answer.

My parents had separated when I was six months old, and I hadn't seen my dad since. He'd been silent, no phone calls or birthday cards for the past 14 years. He'd been driving semi-trucks across the country after the divorce.

With communication severed between my parents, my mom's extended family was all we knew. The only member of my dad's family we'd had any contact with was my great-grandmother — who insisted we refer to her as Granny, and who happened to now be permanently resting in a casket.

Granny was as Southern a belle as they come. She outlived her daughter, Lola, and she'd been kind to my mother after the divorce — staying involved and connected in our lives from a distance. We'd made the trip to Hammond to visit her twice, our last sojourn only being 18 months before.

Granny's neighbor was the one who'd reached out, informing us that the funeral was in two days. Interestingly, we'd heard nothing from my uncle who was organizing the ceremony, and who had a reputation for only looking out for himself. My mother had to make a quick decision with many possible outcomes, ultimately deciding it was best to go and pay our respects to Granny in person. We would let the chips fall where they may with the potential of meeting our father for the first time.

So there we were: three Yankees, out of place in the deep south, trying to organize the chaos inside of ourselves and make it to an 11am funeral on time.

We parked our white rental car and walked into the quiet lobby of the funeral home, late enough to be the last people arriving. Two large, closed, wooden doors separated us from the other mourners in the sanctuary. With wide eyes and an elevated heart rate, I walked through the room, scanning for any familiar faces that might bear a resemblance to mine.

The ceremony had not yet begun, and although most people were seated and all I could see were the backs of their stoic heads, a few were gathered in pockets around the room quietly greeting and exchanging sympathies. Reading the room like a book, I scanned left to right, my eyes landing on a tall man standing on the right side of the sanctuary. He was speaking to another stranger. His dark hair was thick and slicked back, adding a few inches to his already 6'4" frame. He had broad shoulders and glasses, and I noticed his lip pulled to the left as he spoke to the person in front of him.

I slipped my hand under my brother's girthy arm and whispered, "That's him!" subtly pointing to the man I knew must be our father.

It was like seeing a fairytale character come to life. I'd only heard stories of my dad's impressive height and frame., and I'd only seen a few photos. When my mother told him he needed to get some help, he'd rented a U-Haul and taken almost everything left in the house to the dump, pictures and all.

I knew I took after him in many ways. I'd heard of his artistic side, and I identified with that quite a bit, as the rest of my family gravitated more toward science and athletics. But mostly, I'd heard of his height and that one summer when he grew six inches in three months. Like him, I was tall, my 5'9" stature already towering over my mom and brother for years. Oh, how I'd longed for his tall, affirming presence in my life, but he had been absent and silent — leaving me to wonder where I belonged in the family that surrounded me, and with hope for a "someday" when we'd meet. I just never pictured that someday to be at a funeral.

I was old enough to know that two sets of DNA had collided in order to make me, and I was insatiably curious about the set I seemed to resemble yet had never rubbed shoulders with. My whole life, I'd stood out from the people around me, when all I wanted was to blend in. From my height to my wide-set hips and the awkward way I stood, I was unlike anyone else in my family. This moment, seeing him stand with his own feet pointed like a penguin—I felt I belonged with *him*. Seeing him felt as though I was encountering a part of myself that was foreign, a piece of me that had been missing for years.

Noticing the movement in the back of the room upon our entry through the large, wooden doors, my father glanced in our direction. I'd seen him first, so I watched as he looked away quickly, looked back, looked at the floor, and finally looked back at us. I saw his face change, a glimmer of panic and joy. He seemed to look past me, recognizing and fixing his gaze on my mother. Time slowed as my heartbeat drummed in my ears. With my eyes locked on him, it was as though no one else was in the room.

My anticipation grew as I watched him excuse himself from the conversation and move toward us. We were only a few steps inside the sanctuary, frozen as though we'd been following instructions that ended at arrival, and none of us knew what to do next. I took it all in, every second as this man approached. I was 14, and this is what I had dreamt of my whole life. It was like looking in a mirror; he walked just like me, his large frame swaying as he moved closer and closer.

What was this feeling? Until now, my father had been a mythical creature of sorts. But here he was in the flesh, proving that dreams really could, in fact, come true.

His energy was gentle but nervous as he reached us. Still fixed on my mother — as his obsession had always been with her — he greeted her first, awkwardly shaking her hand and saying her name. Next, he shifted to my brother and smiled, their lips curling in the same corner; it was uncanny.

"Hello May-thew," he said with such a southern draw, I almost giggled. They shook hands firmly, like men.

My brother, only 15 at the time, stood strong and confidently with his linebacker build. He responded simply, "Nice to meet you, sir."

My turn! My turn! My turn! My turn! My turn! My insides exploded as I posed, waiting for my turn, my moment, *the moment.*

Finally, he turned his attention toward me. For a delicious moment, I had his full, undivided attention. I hadn't known how hungry I'd been for it until it was here. I savored it and following my brother's polite example, reached out my hand. My father's giant, strong hand swallowed my boney fingers and embraced them in a handshake as we made eye contact for the first time I could remember.

In an instant, my young brain flooded with the burden to 'make the most of this!' I'd waited so long for this moment, and I didn't know when another like it may happen again.

I wonder how long he's staying after the funeral.
How long are we staying?
Will we get to hang out at all?
I think he's going to like Matt and me, he just needs some time to get to know us…

His greeting interrupted my internal monologue. Still shaking his hand, I heard his southern drawl say:

"And you must be Purcella."

….no… No… NO! This is not right. Wait — Does he not know who I am? Has he not imagined this day? Did he only want a son? Why did he know Matt's name and not mine?

Scrambling to breathe, my mind raced. His words landed on me like a sucker punch to the solar plexus, and I frantically searched for a way to rebound. *What should I do? Say something? Run away?*

"No, it's Stephanie," I politely corrected with a wounded smile, as my hand went limp inside of his.

"Oh, that's right!" He chuckled bashfully. "Yeah, okay Stephanie!" He was embarrassed and nervous and none of us had any way of knowing the impact of what had just occurred inside me.

Before another word could be spoken, an usher interrupted, breaking the invisible perimeter of our first-ever family circle, asking the immediate family to please be seated in the front two rows. We followed instructions, grateful for some direction, and moved down the center aisle toward the casket in the front of the room. I fantasized briefly about breaking form and running to the bathroom to kick over some trash cans and scream. Rage and heartache collided within, and I suddenly had the urge to destroy something, even if it was a paper towel. But instead, I felt a dam of tears break inside me the moment my father's back turned. Tears flowed gently and steadily, and I could not stop them.

"I can't sit next to him!" I whispered desperately to Mommy as we filed into the pew, discreetly motioning for her and my brother to switch places with me. Needing as much distance as was socially acceptable in the moment, I sat on the end of the pew, near the aisle, next to the complimentary box of tissues. With my body situated and assigned to a place for the next 45 minutes, the tears shifted from gentle and steady to a shoulder-dancing weep. I sobbed from a depth I didn't know existed in me.

How could this have gone so wrong, already? I wanted a re-do, a do-over. I couldn't accept those as the first words he would say to me. This couldn't be the story; this wasn't how it was supposed to go. I'd spent years choosing to stay positive and patient, trying not to take his silence or absence as a personal slight. I'd surmised that as the years passed, the cavern between us had grown so large that he just didn't know how to cross it. Plus, he'd not known what he was missing, and if he was just given the opportunity to meet me, he'd see how much I was like him, he'd be proud of me, and he'd want me. But this—calling me by my cousin's name, a cousin whom I'd never met — didn't fit my narrative. Maybe he just plain didn't want me? Maybe his silence all those years had been because he preferred to live as though I didn't exist. Maybe he hadn't thought of me at all.

When an exorbitant gasp for air came in between blunders, I assumed people would just chalk it up to a devoted granddaughter grieving, until my mother touched my knee and quietly said, "Steph, pull it together."

Although I know it was not her intention, at that moment, I understood her to say I was 'too much,' and once again, I tried to become small. I resented the bigness of the frame I inhabited and the bigness of spirit that was inside of it. I felt embarrassed and ashamed, both that my father didn't seem to know me, and that I apparently was supposed to be more put together about it. I looked around the room, suddenly aware of my surroundings, and observed the subtle southern etiquette that — even at a funeral — one cannot grieve too deeply. So, I tried to suffocate my sadness.

***

Meeting again in Granny's estate the following day, we rummaged through a few belongings, and I studied every part of my dad. I folded my legs, sitting on the carpet near his bare feet, observing the gap between his big toe and index toe that resembled mine. I had a soft spot for him, he was clumsy and awkward, but kind and earnest in his attempts to please.

The dynamic was fascinating between my dad and his younger brother, Steve. Even at 14, I could sense that Steve was a slippery character. His ego was inflated, and he was a charmer, working his charisma to get anything and everything he wanted. My dad had an innocence and sincerity about him, and I could tell Steve had mastered the art of manipulating him over the course of their shared life together.

When it was time to leave, I felt my ends begin to fray. Nothing was hemmed in. We didn't have a plan for if, or when, we were going to see each other next. I wasn't ready to say goodbye; I hadn't gotten my fill, it wasn't enough.

My brother shook our dad's hand and moved out of the way so I could say my goodbyes. I threw my arms around his large frame and collapsed into him. It was foreign to feel small in an embrace, and I devoured it for a few short seconds, until my dad began to move away. First, his arms went limp, like wet spaghetti noodles, hinting that he was finished with me. When I tightened my grip on him, communicating I wasn't done, he pushed me away and said, "That's enough now."

I began to cry, feeling rejected and embarrassed as Mommy shielded half her face with her hand, giving her ex some side-eye and whispering, "Just hold her, Scott."

He attempted a side hug with me, finishing with a shoulder pat before releasing me again quickly. I could tell he was looking for Mommy's approval, not mine. He turned his attention toward her, leaning in for a hug, but she walked past him, strictly offering a verbal goodbye as we made our way to our rental car.

When the door closed, I fell apart. I sobbed because I'd seen a glimpse of how broken it all was, and I couldn't fix it. The curtain which had shielded me in childhood innocence had been pulled back. I'd been introduced to the complexity and nuance that existed within every person. It was clear to me that my dad wasn't a bad man, but did that make him a good one? I could see his desire for my mom, but I wanted it to be for me. Maybe we just needed more time? I'd been told he was bi-polar, and likely schizophrenic, with severe social anxiety. But did his sickness excuse him from the hurt and anger I felt not having a father? Who was at fault here? And who was going to fix this?

I didn't have a category for any of it. It was all so complicated. I was drawn to him and felt tender towards him—like he was a little boy himself, earnestly trying to do his best in the world—yet I felt rejected and unknown by him, hurt to a depth I didn't know existed in me. I couldn't make sense of what was happening inside me. Disappointed by expectations I hadn't realized I'd even had, I found comfort in going home to what felt safe and familiar.

***

The day after we got back, I was eating an afternoon bowl of cereal as I made my way down the stairs to our newly renovated basement. My brother was on the desktop computer, chatting on Instant Messenger, and he got prickly when I entered the room.

"Steph, go away. Stay over there."

"What? Who are you talking to?"

"I'm talking to your asshole boyfriend, Chris; stay over there."

"Tell him I said hi! What are you guys talking about?"

"Steph—seriously!" Matt said, typing ferociously.

Earning my badge as an annoying little sister, I disregarded his instructions and stood over his shoulder, looking at the IBM screen and chewing cereal loudly in his ear.

Throwing his hands in the air, Matt exhaled loudly. He motioned for me to sit in the chair he was exiting. "Here, you talk to him."

Trying to get my bearings, as Matt's annoyance level was higher than usual with me, I skimmed the few lines of their conversation that I could see.

Mattman95: She's standing right here. You tell her or I will
UhlDawg: Dude…
Mattman95: Here she is
UhlDawg: Ok fine

I looked at Matt, pleading for context, as he softened towards me. "You talk to him, I'll leave you," he said, heading upstairs.

Sitting in an oversized computer chair, chatting through my big brother's IM name, my first boyfriend broke up with me. It was two weeks after my first kiss, and two days after returning home from Granny's funeral. After telling him about meeting my dad for the first time, I'd assumed that he'd comfort me and assure me how much he "loved" me—to the best of his 15-year-old abilities. I certainly hadn't braced for another rejection.

I had just wanted things to go back to normal. But returning home, I couldn't find normal anymore.

Chapter 2
Pain Reveals Passion

After the funeral, life appeared to be moving on, but as the spring semester of my freshman year began, Mommy was noticing some changes in me. I was gaining weight, I'd grown lethargic and lost interest in social activities and friends, and my grades were dropping. She'd heard the rumors of mono going around the school, so her first swing at finding answers was to schedule a checkup with our family practitioner.

Sitting in the sterile exam room waiting for the results of the mono test, I just knew I had it. After all, it was called the kissing disease, and I had officially been kissed — never mind that it had been months ago.

My doctor entered the room and led with the positive. "Good news: You don't have mono!" But before I could be completely relieved, I noticed a pamphlet in his hands. Taking a seat on a round rolling stool, he slid toward me, handing me the small, folded piece of paper as he gently said, "But I'd like to talk to you about clinical depression."

Shame and fear flooded me. *Was I mentally ill like my dad? How embarrassing. Why couldn't I just bounce back? None of my friends were experiencing this; was I a freak?* But truth be told, I was also relieved. Not only did I not know how to heal from my first broken heart, but also, after the impact of a double whammy rejection, maybe I did need some help.

The doctor explained we could take one of two routes, meds or talk therapy. I chose therapy and began to see a child psychologist. She helped explain my dad's illness to me, helped me understand it wasn't about me, and that sick people acted sick. She also took interest in me and asked questions like, "What do you like to do?" that led to self-discovery.

Growing up, I was an introverted and shy little girl, happy to let Matt be the loud one with an opinion on everything. I found it hard to trust myself and even harder to speak up. Although I had a strong intuition and knew what I liked and wanted, I was easily overpowered by others, who I assumed knew more than me—like my neighbor friend, Ashley, who dialed my sixth-grade crush, Kirk, and handed me the phone once he'd answered, insisting it was a great idea to tell him that I liked him. Turns out, it wasn't a great idea, and I didn't like feeling pressured into it, but I didn't know how to stand my ground. I nervously confessed my mega-crush. Immediately, thinking he'd hung up because the line fell silent, I squabbled a panicked "Hello?!" After a long, awkward pause, I heard him say "I'm here." He didn't hang up; he just didn't know what to say. Thankfully, he was gracious and still said hi to me in the hallways, even if it was out of courtesy.

The world was big and scary to me. I preferred to live in my colorful interior world, playing dress up, drawing, painting, coloring, building, writing, all the while imagining and rehearsing what I would do someday when I was ready. I knew there were parts of me undiscovered, and it would take time to find them. I think I even knew I would have to step out of my comfort zone to find them. I just didn't know how to move the mountain of fear and social anxiety that sat on my chest.

One snowy Pennsylvania afternoon, when I was six or so, Mommy took us to an open gym day at Rec Hall on the Penn State campus where kids could play on some of the University's gymnastics equipment. Parents sat on wooden bleachers from the 50's, keeping watchful eyes on their littles as they burned off the combustible energy stored within their tiny frames.

Matt handed off his coat and gloves before we even entered the gym. For him, the clock was ticking and not a second of precious playtime was to be wasted. He gleefully, without reservation, entered and indulged in all that was offered to him.

But I sat glued to Mommy's side because the thought of jumping right in like my brother had done—so stinking effortlessly—made me panic. I needed to be a wallflower, observe the room, gauge the temperature, and assess the other kids from a distance to see if one might appear safe enough for potential friendship.

Occasionally, I'd look up and watch the other kids playing. I noticed Matt had made a friend, and they looked like they were having fun.

Try it out, I thought. *It looks fun.*

Even though part of me wanted to try, I didn't even know how to begin to participate.

After nearly two hours of sitting quietly and watching the fun happen right before my eyes, I tapped Mommy's knee timidly.

"Mommy," I whispered. "I'm ready to go play now."

My mother looked baffled. She graciously said, "Oh sweetie, I'm sorry but it's ending. They're cleaning up, and it's time for us to go home now."

As tears persisted, I tried to problem solve and manipulate the situation to get my way. "Can I play for just a few minutes?" I asked, panic rising.

Again, looking at the gym floor, then back at me, my mom tried to muster some sympathy despite confusion over my tardy change of heart. "No honey, I'm sorry, but it's over now," and with a gentle sternness she added, "You had a lot of time to decide differently."

With time, I realized I just needed a little more practice than others at moving from observation to participation. Eventually, I began to decide differently, and I learned how to participate with the adventure happening right in front of me. Because after all, no one can participate for you.

But being as shy as I was back then, most of my hobbies were introverted in nature, more artistic and creative than the team sports pastimes of my brother, but I had just started going to a new youth group per my mother's insistent nudging. I hadn't been able to muster the courage to go without a friend, so I'd suckered my neighbor into joining me. I really liked the music there; they had a full band, and they let some of the kids sing sometimes. I had privately hoped I could find the nerve to ask to sing there someday. I felt safe with my psychologist, so I shared my dream of singing with her — something not many people knew.

I had two close friends in high school, Kylene and Liz, and we did our own thing. We weren't super popular, but we weren't on the bottom end of the social rejects either. We were in on the Emo/Pop Punk scene when everyone else seemed to be wearing Abercrombie & Fitch though, and we loved music. I envied how easily both Kylene and Liz could take the stage and command an audience. It wasn't natural for me, one of the only ways I felt comfortable expressing myself publicly was through my outfits. Before I could walk or talk, I was fussy about what Mommy dressed me in, and in high school, I discovered the joys of thrifting. Grandma Billie asked my mom if I needed money to buy a new coat one winter because I kept bringing home thrifted jackets. Mommy had to explain to my sweet grandmother that I liked them because they were weird. Or "scene" if you would've asked me at the time.

When I was six, I attempted "O Christmas Tree' as a duet with Mommy, but it wasn't much of a duet. I'd ended up hiding behind her floral dress as she sang it, apologizing to the audience with her eyes for her clearly distraught daughter. I'd started crying before I even got on stage, scared to tears, and my tender Mommy assured me I didn't have to do it. Through my sobs, I insisted I still wanted to, so I'd taken the stage with her and survived the three minutes of terror, but we hadn't tried much singing since then.

After a few months of meeting weekly, my therapist told Mommy that she didn't think I needed to see her anymore, but in the exit meeting, she asked, "Did you know when Stephanie talks about music, it's as though someone turned on a light switch inside of her?" Mommy was surprised — not that I loved to sing, but that I might want to do it in front of living, breathing, souls. The therapist suggested if I ever showed an interest in pursuing music, to encourage it. Even though I didn't yet know how to share it with the world, she could see that at least privately, singing was an other-worldly experience for me.

That same year, Grandma Billie presented me with a generous offer. She wanted to invest in my love for music somehow and offered to either buy me a new flute—indeed, I was a super cool band geek—or voice lessons for a year. I listened to the growing passion inside of me, even though it scared me to death, and I chose voice lessons.

All I wanted to do was sing. Youth group culture had introduced me to a popular 90's Christian band, dcTalk. I'd worn their cassette tapes thin, developing my ear with each rewind and replay, identifying the string parts, bass lines, and most importantly, vocal harmonies as I'd followed the moody vibrato of Kevin Max and soulful croons of Michael Tait. As high school progressed, I'd mustered the courage to begin singing in my youth group. My youth pastor, Jonathan Weibel —who would walk me down the aisle at my wedding one day—was also a musician and he saw something hidden within me and patiently invested in encouraging it out of me. Timidly, I would sing backup vocals standing two feet away from the mic, afraid of the sound of my own voice. But over time, I completely fell in love with it, and eventually, would need to be encouraged to back off the mic. It was clear — there was nothing else I wanted to do with my life.

Naturally, as a card-carrying Christian music enthusiast, I was a subscriber to CCM magazine. One day, towards the end of my junior year, an edition arrived with Jars of Clay on the cover, advertising Greenville College, a tiny liberal arts school in the middle of nowhere, with a question: "Want to Jump Start Your Music Career While Earning Your College Degree?" *Check yes. Count me all in.*

It was a bold move for me to relocate 13 hours away. I had originally thought if I even went to college, it would be close enough for me to come home for weekend visits as I was quite attached to my family and friends. My high school, neighboring Penn State, was huge and I got lost in the waters. I needed a smaller pond, more like the youth group setting I had thrived in. So that's what I did. I moved across the country to a corn field with a small, liberal arts college placed in the middle of it. And it didn't take long at all before my shy exterior faded and the whimsical and quirky personality that had been hiding within erupted.

To some degree, it was sink or swim, so swam I did — but it also became a learned survival technique. I discovered I could win others over with my new enthusiastic, sparkly, shiny, and outgoing persona. The problem I wouldn't be aware of for years to come was: if I won them over when I was "on," what would happen if I ever needed to turn "off"? The second semester of my freshman year at college, I was asked to be in a band with several upperclassmen guys. We gained momentum quickly, and I felt like I was doing what I was made to do; I felt alive. I had never been part of any kind of band outside of my youth worship band, so I figured I would fake it until I made it in my new role as front woman.

Except for our guitar player, Joe, the guys were often critical and cold towards me, a freshman who didn't know what she was doing. They had years of experience on me and felt the ticking clock of their senior year ending and the real world knocking. But Joe was more like a big brother, a mentor of sorts. He made me feel seen and safe. Together we were all excited to make something of ourselves, so when Joe confessed his feelings for me, things got complicated—most importantly because Joe was married.

It was the summer after my freshman year and as a band, we had all decided to stay in the sleepy town of Greenville, Illinois to make a go of the band full-time. I had no friends other than my bandmates, most of whom I was convinced only tolerated me. I didn't have feelings for Joe, there was no future I could see romantically for us, but I was also lonely and didn't want him to leave the band because he made me feel safe. He was the one who provided me with a sense of belonging; I just wanted things to go back to when he felt like a big brother. But big brothers didn't try to sneak into your room at night. I was 18 and not used to having friends who were married. I handled the whole thing with the maturity of a teenager and passively told him nothing could happen between us; we should just continue as normal band-mates. But Joe persisted and I found myself in sticky situations, one after another, until it all blew up. Rumors flew, most of them not true, but I had participated by trying to manage and control perceptions and outcomes, all the while keeping the truth disguised. What had been hidden needed to come to light. Joe and his wife needed to focus on their relationship, and I needed to get out of the way and let them do so. Even if it meant losing the band.

As quickly as we rose, we fell. The whole band disintegrated, and it wrecked me, both breaking my heart and scaring me. I was humiliated and didn't like who I'd become. Keeping the band going had gained precedence over my ability to stay true to myself. When I became aware of how I'd prioritized the approval of others, I decided music turned me into someone I didn't like. I didn't yet understand that the wounds of my barely finished childhood had left me starving for affirmation and validation, so much so that I would allow myself to get hooked to any source that provided a taste of it. In my black and white thinking at the time, I assumed music was the problem. And I gave it up altogether by the beginning of my sophomore year, withdrawing from all my music classes and changing my major to "undecided."

Suddenly directionless, I decided to do a little soul searching, and in January of 2004, I signed up for a three-week block course to Guatemala with my favorite teacher, Professor Houston, to knock out some history gen-eds.

I was taken with the vibrant color of Guatemalan culture, and grateful for the opportunity to see beyond my self-absorbed, 19-year-old bubble. As I helped haul cinder blocks up a mountain in a rural area to build safe stoves for an impoverished community, I experienced the sincere gratitude from an entire village for the ability to cook food safely and nourish their family, something I had completely taken for granted. I realized I'd arrived with the mindset that I was coming to help them, but really, it was my own heart that needed help. I discovered the best medicine for anyone preoccupied with their own problems was to serve someone else.

Returning home from the life-changing trip, I landed in Chicago and called Mommy from a payphone to let her know I was back on American soil. She was glad to hear from me—we'd been traveling for several days without Wi-Fi in a pre-iPhone world—but she also had some time-sensitive news to deliver. One of my student loans had not been approved and she was tapped out financially on parental loans. With the spring semester of my sophomore year set to begin in three days, she told me I had two options. 1) Move home to Pennsylvania for the semester and work to save up to return in the fall, or 2) Call my dad and see if he would be willing to help.

I felt a tingle travel down my arms and a flutter in my tummy. *Call my dad?* I thought excitedly. Other than the graduation card telling me of my grandfather's death, I hadn't heard a peep from him in five years. I had thought a lot about reaching out to him, but I only mustered the courage to bring it up to Mommy once or twice.

Her response was always the same, "When you're 18, if you want a relationship with him, you can do that then. Your dad isn't a bad man, but he is a complicated man, and I think it'd be better if you were older."

I hadn't thought about it much since I'd turned 18. I'd been busy trying to be a rockstar who had a quick and clumsy fall from grace. But now, here Mommy was, actually suggesting that I reach out to him! I wrote down his phone number in my journal and decided I would call from a quieter place when I had my wits about me.

Since the dorms weren't open yet, I accepted a friend's invitation to stay at his parents' house in St. Louis for a night. I had the guest room to myself, and once I'd settled in, with Guatemalan soil still on my shoes, I stared at my open flip phone, willing myself to dial my dad's number. If he answered, this would be the second time in my life we would ever speak to each other.

I couldn't think too much about it. I needed to know if he was willing and/or able to contribute to my education by taking out a parental loan. If not, I'd be moving home in 24 hours. I hit send. It rang.

As it rang a second time, I imagined him answering, and it occurred to me: *What do I call him? Scott? Dad?* —

"Hello?" A southern drawl pulled the end of the word upward like a question.

Say something, initiate prepared speech, NOW.

"Dad, this is Stephanie."

"Who?" he asked, not understanding.

"It's, um, Stephanie, your daughter?" I said, finishing the statement with my own raised pitch.

"Ohhh! Okay, yeah, ya caught me off guard! I got ya now," he chuckled, perhaps embarrassed.

I considered being offended that once again he hadn't recognized me immediately; it felt just like the last time. But I knew I was disrupting his evening, unannounced, and perhaps it was a little surprising to hear from me. I also knew if I wavered, the tears would overtake me, so I started in with urgency.

"I'm calling because my mom just told me that I don't have enough money for school this semester. I'm in college in Illinois, but I've been in Guatemala for the past three weeks, and she hasn't been able to get a hold of me, so, um, I'm sorry it's so last minute, but I need some money for this semester, or else I have to move home to Pennsylvania in the next two days, and I was just wondering if maybe you could help?" My tears broke through, and I barely squeaked out the request before I paused to come up for air.

Taking advantage of my need to collect myself, my dad interjected. "Okay, slow down now. What's going on?" he said in his long southern drawl, still trying to wrap his head around not only the surprise of my call, but the request that was being made of him.

I took a deep breath, drew on what courage I could muster to ask again, and slowed down as I repeated what felt pertinent.

"How much are we talking here?" he asked.

"I need $3,000 for this semester. You can file for a parental loan; I have all the information for you — and I will pay you back if you want — but you'd have to do it by tomorrow." I winced, wondering how that number and deadline landed on him, embarrassed that I couldn't disguise my tears as they reappeared.

"Aw, now don't cry," he continued slowly, warmer now. "Okay, I can probably do that. You said you have the number for me to call?"

Once I gave him all the relevant info that Mommy had given me to pass on, he shifted the conversation, asking if the number I was calling from was my cell phone. He wanted to save it and expressed interest in trying to stay in touch. Cue my insides melting.

I had hardly been able to imagine a world where we had any communication. We didn't have photos or shared memories together. We had one encounter at a funeral that hadn't gone very well — and yet I'd never lost hope. Something in me knew he would be part of my life someday.

I knew he was enough of a wild card not to get too excited, but I was up for the adventure of trying. I was slightly aware of the comfortable balance we might be upsetting by traveling down this road, but I was determined to see how it all played out.

Sure enough, he followed through on the loan and called me the next day to announce that he'd got it all sorted out. He also mentioned how nice it had been to hear from me and asked again where I was going to college. I told him it was right off I-70, about 45 miles east of St. Louis.

"That's what I thought you said!" he exclaimed, seemingly relieved, as though he couldn't remember if he'd made it up. Or maybe he was nervous and looking for a way out of what he was about to suggest, because the next thing he said was brave.

"Well, I'm still driving for JB Hunt, and I have a truck route taking me right through there on I-70 next Thursday. I was thinking, if you knew of a truck stop somewhere near your school, maybe we could meet for lunch or something?"

I felt my heart expand within me and simultaneously turn to mush.

My Father — initiating?
He wanted to see me?!
Dreams really do come true!

I could barely contain myself, and I knew of just the place to meet.

The Powhatan was a 24-hour diner attached to a motel with truck parking, about 20 minutes from campus. Greenville College students affectionately called it "Pokey" because it was in the neighboring town of Pocahontas and provided an all-hours escape from campus. At any given hour of the night, a car full of students could be found squeezing into a booth and sharing a basket of chicken tenders. Not to mention the infamous "Ooey Gooey," an opulently large, fudge brownie dessert that couldn't be finished alone and was therefore an accomplice in me gaining the freshman 15… on a budget.

I told my dad about Pokey and suggested we meet there. He asked me to email him the address when I could find it, and I agreed to. My heart raced. In five short days, we would be face-to-face again for the second time. I had a sociology class on Thursdays that ended at 11am, and although I don't remember much about the class specifically, I remember where I sat in the room, and the questions that consumed my attention that day.

Would he show? Would he recognize me? What would we talk about? Would he like me? Did I even want him to come? This all felt risky. What would this new relationship look like? Did I actually want this?

I didn't know how to identify what was going on inside of me. Words like ambivalence were not yet in my vocabulary, and I didn't know it was possible to both want this new relationship and be scared at the same time. It felt wild, untamed, and unpredictable. I had a feeling that I didn't know what a relationship with this man would require of me, and that both intimidated and intrigued me. I did have a sense, just from our brief phone conversations, that I would be the leader of our new dynamic though.

I knew my dad struggled with mental illness, and sometimes acted irrationally, but I wasn't scared of him. My mom had assured me he wasn't dangerous, however she was well acquainted with his impulsive and erratic communication style and feared he would hurt me emotionally. While I was under her roof, she saw her job as my protector, and she had taken that job very seriously. She'd wanted my brother and I to have more consistency than he could offer, so she had acted as a gatekeeper in the beginning, but it hadn't been long before my dad stopped trying all together. Eventually there was no gate to keep, it collapsed into a canyon so vast, no one knew how to cross it.

Until now.

Chapter 3
We All Come from Somewhere

In 1984, something catapulted me into existence. I could not be stopped. I was not planned or expected—or arguably wanted—when my embryonic presence was made known. So much so, that a doctor suggested to my mother that she consider an abortion, and for a moment, she did. My parents' marriage was unraveling, and my older brother was only five months old when the pregnancy test read positive. They already had their hands full between a newborn, a chaotic marriage, and rubbing pennies together to survive while living in a tiny, scorpion-infested apartment in Tulsa.

After dropping out of the Bible school that had prompted their move to the Sooner State in the first place, my dad was working odd shifts at a gas station, stealing Snickers to quiet his hungry belly, and keeping an IOU tab by the cash register to quiet his guilty conscience. He was also trying to pray away the growing imbalance in his brain chemistry that was only just beginning.

Because of the circumstances, the energy with which I was welcomed into the world was *you're not really wanted here*. And I would spend the first act of my life trying to outrun that initial welcome. My parents met in Marion, VA, in 1980, when my mom moved to take a job after graduating as a dietitian from Penn State. She was nursing a broken heart as the seven-year relationship with her high school / college boyfriend had recently dissolved. At 23, she was beginning to feel like an old maid as her sisters had married, respectively at 18 and 19 – and were already a few babies deep into motherhood.

My father was a newly converted Christian and was "on fire" for the Lord. He saw my cute little mommy and just couldn't help himself; he was smitten. Tall and handsome, but a little socially awkward, he was endearing and pursued her in a clumsy, charming, southern boy way that made her feel seen and special. When my dad casually proposed after a few months of dating, without a ring or a plan, she accepted — maybe out of love, maybe out of fear that there wouldn't be any other options — either way, it was a fast courtship. Two broken people in their twenties, not knowing what they didn't know, married in December of 1980.

Only two weeks into marriage, Mommy had the first flash of *Oh no, what have I done* cross her mind. My father lost his temper when a lid from a pot hit him in the face after he turned it on its side, removing it from a shelf Mommy couldn't reach. Because she'd made the request of him, obviously it was her fault. He lost his mind for a moment, terrifying his new bride who didn't know what to do but apologize, until he eventually returned to his normal, gentle, and passive self. He knew he'd overreacted but didn't know what to do except beat himself up for it, now positioning his wife as a rescuer and peace-keeper — trying to help him balance out from the dramatic pendulum swing and the inevitable shame that came with the outburst.

Shortly after that incident, he spent more and more time secluded, praying, obsessing, and praying more. One morning, he emerged with what he called a "revelation from God." He announced to his new wife that God told him he was not supposed to have gotten married. Again, she didn't know what to do… but apologize. Meanwhile, suffering from her own confusion from this new epiphany "from God," she couldn't receive it as anything but a rejection. Conflicted by her understanding of the husband being the head of the household, she tried to make sense out of his nonsense and bring order to the growing chaos at home.

This set the tone for the next four years. When it was good, it was sweet, and I believe they really did love each other. But when it was bad, together, both of my parents participated in an unhealthy pattern that only intensified as time went by. My mom, not fully knowing who she was or what she deserved, accepted my dad's growing manic/depressive swings as "something she'd caused." My dad, optimistically believing that his newfound religion would heal him from his undiagnosed mental illness and unresolved childhood trauma, often confused God's voice for an imbalance in his own brain chemistry.

Like a frog in boiling water, my mom struggled to be objective or have perspective as the unhealthy situation heated. After all, the normal we grow accustomed to is, well, normal to us. As is common with mental illness in one's mid-20's, the chemical imbalance in my dad's brain had intensified over the four years they'd been together, but it was gradual, and neither my mother, nor my father, knew exactly what they were dealing with.

Eventually, my brave mother began to wake up. She began seeking help, determined there were more options available other than 'grin and bear it.' She asked a pastor for guidance and after listening to her for a while, he said, "You are not a very submissive wife. You need to go home and submit to your husband." Unfortunately, she had tried that, and it wasn't working—she was only losing herself more and more in her apologies and overcorrections. So, she continued in her pursuit of wellness. After a few other shitty advice-givers, more or less suggesting she just "pray harder," someone finally spoke her language. She met with a counselor who offered the context she could understand.

"You're a dietitian, correct? You help people nourish their bodies. Maybe your soul needs some nourishment. Is there a safe place you can go, where your soul can be fed for a while?"

Now that was an analogy she could understand. She planned a trip for three—one adult, an almost-toddler, and a six-month-old infant— to visit her parents in her hometown, State College, Pennsylvania. My dad cautiously agreed to let her go, also knowing things weren't going well between them. The trip was slightly open-ended, because a return ticket was not necessary in 1984, but the general understanding was she'd be gone for ten days or so.

As the trip approached, my dad's anxiety grew, and my mom began to worry that he would try to stop her from going. One evening just before the trip, my dad was studying in the kitchen. My mother, being a die-hard Penn State fan, had the game on in the den, and it became a distraction to my dad. He asked her to turn it off. She muted the game, assuming it'd have the same impact for him being in another room.

The growing chaos in my father's own mind was already too much for him, on top of a fussy toddler, a newborn, and the pressures of work. He was at his limit, and he snapped. Not knowing how to take care of himself, let alone his family, perhaps he believed the noise in his own mind would quiet down if the TV was off. His obsession with getting his way grew, and logic left the building. The only communication he had in that moment was violence.

Mommy, tending to my brother Matt, picked him up and was holding him when my dad approached her in his anger. They exchanged words as he stormed into the living room and came after her, cornering her to fall into a chair while holding Matt. Seeing the rage in his eyes, and with her arms already assigned to protecting her baby boy, she used her leg to keep him at a distance. In his rage, he grabbed it and pulled, dragging her out of the chair and onto the carpet. Still holding Matt, she used her elbows as brakes as my father dragged her across the room, bloodying her from carpet burn.

A few days later, with $50 in her pocket, she juggled two babies, one suitcase, and a diaper bag through a layover in the Pittsburgh airport—eventually arriving at her parents' home. My grandma Billie was excited to have us and get some quality time with her two newest grandchildren. Of course, at the time, none of us knew we'd be house guests for the foreseeable future.

The day after we arrived, my grandmother spotted Mommy's scabbed elbows and asked her what happened. Chaos and fear, combined with a high priority on keeping the peace, had become constant companions for Mommy at this point, so without thinking, she lied to her own mother and told her she'd fallen down the stairs. But it only took a half glass of wine the next night at dinner for Mommy to clear her guilty conscience—she's always been a lightweight. When Grandma Billie learned of my father's aggression, every ounce of her 60 inches multiplied with authority as she announced, "If you want to go back there, fine, but you are not taking my grandchildren with you."

It was October 1984. The same month a movie starring Farrah Fawcett called "The Burning Bed" was released, in which she portrays a woman suffering from domestic violence who pours gasoline over her sleeping husband and lights him on fire to make that chaos stop. For the first time, Mommy was able to see her own rage and recognize that something had to change. Sometimes we must see ourselves portrayed somewhere else in order to make the connection within.

Believing my father was a sick man, not a bad man, she told him she'd return to Tulsa on one condition: that he agreed to both couples and individual therapy. Hoping her marriage could be saved, she temporarily left my brother and I in Pennsylvania with my grandparents, while she flew back to Oklahoma.

My dad was the firstborn of two boys. Steve, the younger brother, quickly became their mother's favorite, and my dad learned early that he didn't belong. His mother, Lola, came from money and class but suffered from severe undiagnosed mental illness. For years, she was untreated because it was frowned upon to speak of, look at, or acknowledge things like mental illness, let alone seek treatment for such things. Eventually, later in her life, doctors threw medicine at her until she was a zombie and her family learned to walk on eggshells around her. Ultimately, she was diagnosed with severe paranoid schizophrenia and bipolar disorder. I never met her. She took her own life in 1993, when I was in third grade. My dad had not made an appearance at her funeral. At the time, I was pulled out of my third-grade class to see the school counselor. I think someone simply told me her heart stopped, and I cried because I never got to meet her.

My dad's father, Jerry, was an architect and couldn't bear working for other people. He was continually trying to live up to the standards of the family he'd married into, prematurely starting his own firm and going bankrupt twice. He self-medicated with alcohol and abused it until his eventual death from it in 2002, the same year I graduated high school. Just like my grandma Lola, I never met Jerry. I learned of his death in a graduation card from my dad. He wrote telling me Jerry had locked himself in the guest room at his house — on Dad's birthday — and drank himself to death just to spite him after they'd had an argument. Interestingly, my brother had graduated the year before, and a $1,000 check fell out of his card from our Dad, reinforcing my fear (much like at Granny's funeral) that his rejection was unique to me.

As a young man himself trying to earn at least one of his parents' love (since Lola was clearly infatuated with Steve), my dad decided to follow his father's career aspirations and went to Virginia Tech to study architecture.

It was in college, in his early 20's, when he had his first hallucination. Around the same time, he had a religious conversion, and that

27

muddied the waters for him—how could he discern what was God's voice and what was his unbalanced brain playing tricks on him? He'd lived with a front row seat to his mother's struggle with her mental health and didn't want doctors pumping him full of drugs like he'd observed them do with her, so he began to pray that God would take away his mental illness. He was taught and encouraged by authorities in his new belief system, that if you "name it and claim it" God will do it for you. And if you're not getting well, then you must be demonstrating a lack of faith, and you just need to pray harder. So, pray harder he did, as well as stay away from doctors and the medication he so desperately needed.

When Mommy returned to Tulsa—sans kids—and my dad picked her up from the airport, he told her how glad he was she'd come back to him. He never mentioned or asked about his children, as his fixation was always on her. His tormented mind and un-mothered heart likely felt a sense of serenity when she was home with him and therefore, by proximity, he felt affirmed as lovable. He had never been taught love, he didn't know it was free and couldn't be manipulated, so when he experienced a taste of it, naturally, his grip tightened, and he desperately grasped to control it and keep it.

When it came time for the promised couples therapy, my dad dragged his feet but knew it had been part of the agreement, so he went to the first appointment to be a good sport. The counselor wanted to see them first alone, then together. Feeling optimistic because of her husband's participation, and safe to speak candidly because she was alone, Mommy poured out her heart, not holding back, finally ready to face the mountain in front of her head on.

The therapist told her—under no uncertain terms—that there were five things my dad needed to follow through on consistently before it would be safe for her and the children to even consider returning to living in the home. He made sure she understood that if my dad failed to do even one of the five, it was not wise or safe to return home.

After the appointment, Mommy asked my dad what he thought and he scoffed "I'm not doing any of that, I just said I'd go to get you back here." Heartbroken, my mother began to accept that her marriage was over.

A healthy relationship doesn't happen by accident. It takes two willing people to be well. One cannot bend or manipulate another person's will. Sometimes you must realize that you are participating in the chaos by staying. Ultimately, as my mother's heart broke over becoming a statistic of divorce, she sensed the gracious, loving, and kind voice of God whisper to her, "Right now, I am more interested in saving three lives than ruining four."

Mommy returned to her babies in Pennsylvania, and we began a new life from her one suitcase, and $50 shoved in her pocket that October day when we left for a visit to Grandma and Grandpa's.

Even as a baby, I was sensitive to the energy around me. Mommy warned Grandma Billie that I was a terrible baby—that I wouldn't sleep or eat, and I was always fussy. But when we arrived in Pennsylvania, I made a liar out of my mom. Sleeping 13 hours a night and eating like a champ, I was a happy baby… at least in Grandma Billie's house. I think I could sense the tension between my parents in Tulsa and had no other way to communicate yet, so I responded to the discord I sensed by contributing to it.

At first, my dad refused to sign the divorce papers. The separation lasted for nearly two years as Mommy continued her education at Penn State and began working at the local hospital. We lived with my grandparents, rebuilding our life one yard sale at a time, until enough was saved to put a deposit down and sign a lease on a townhouse on Southgate Drive. We used food stamps, government assistance, and the generosity of others to get by, but we were safe, and we were happy.

One day, unannounced, the divorce papers arrived, signed. Mommy was shocked. Until this point, my dad had been adamantly against it. What had changed? Who could know? But here they were—perhaps signed in a moment of defeat, possibly acceptance—staring her back in the face.

Custody wasn't going to be an issue. My dad had not even appeared at the custody hearing, so with one knock of the gavel, the judge assigned full custody to Mommy. I wouldn't know it for years to come, but his lack of pursuit, fight, or effort would come to haunt me as the years of his silence grew. *Did he not care? Did he not want me? What made him give up so easily?* I wouldn't find out until years later.

Chapter 4
My Dad Broke Up With Me

Maybe my parents couldn't figure it out, but I was now a (barely) legal adult and finding myself more determined than ever to build a bridge. Clearly, my dad hadn't been able to fix things on his own, he'd been silent for 19 years, but today was a new day. He and I had never tried this on our own and with the opportunity presenting itself, I was fully committed. I wasn't angry with him; I had always been predominantly curious more than anything. Something deep within me knew his silence was more about him than me. The assumption I made — much like leading up to the funeral — was that he just needed a chance to get to know me, and then he would be inspired to participate in our relationship. Maybe I had been too young before, maybe he wasn't ready four years ago, but maybe today he was.

If nothing else, I was encouraged by his initiating this meeting. Perhaps I was looking for the silver lining, or perhaps I wanted to manage my expectations so as to not be terribly let down. Regardless, after nearly two decades of emotional starvation, I was unaware that I was worthy of a feast. I was simply grateful for the breadcrumbs offered to me.

Heading west on I-70, I put my favorite MxPx CD in my portable Discman — that plugged into a cassette tape adapter. Despite the back right speaker being blown, I turned it up, heart beating like Yuri's machine gun kickdrum, and I sang along to calm my nerves.

As I pulled into the familiar, front parking lot at Pokey, I looked nervously in the direction of the truck parking area to see if I could locate a JB Hunt semi. It was hard to tell from where I was, so I knew I had to enter to find out if he'd come or not.

Walking through the glass doors, I scanned the room, quickly landing my gaze on a large man seated at a small table towards the back of the restaurant. He wore overalls, and the same thick glasses I remembered from the funeral, slid down his dominant nose as he examined the menu. I'd know him anywhere.

As I approached the table, he looked up and smiled adorably at me, communicating that he did in fact recognize me. He seemed genuinely happy to see me, and he took his time taking me in.

"Wow," he said, admiring me as I sat down and joined him at the tiny table, "You're all grown up." He smirked a boyish smile and added, "This is so cool," his long southern drawl immediately welcoming.

He ordered a Cobb salad with extra ranch dressing. Shoveling forkfuls of lettuce into his mouth like a teenage boy, and talking with his mouthful, at one point a little of the extra ranch ended up on his chin. He was so endearing. I had such a soft spot for him.

Even at 19, I sensed this visit was incredibly brave for him. To emerge from the isolated environment he had orchestrated for himself, driving trucks and living alone, to sit with me, his daughter, a stranger to him, took great effort on his part. I related to his social anxieties. I, too, had been such a shy kid, afraid of the world and unsure how to engage with it. But unlike him, I had begun to outgrow it. I had continued to place myself in situations where I had to practice how to show up and participate with people, places, and things that scared me or challenged me. Over time, I was beginning to collect evidence that my biggest fears wouldn't actually kill me if I faced them. Instead, they would be a conduit for my growth.

I'd printed off some pictures from Guatemala to show him, and I told him about my trip. We small talked for a bit, and eventually, it was time to wrap up because I had an afternoon class. Mommy had suggested I have him look at the tires on my car while we were together. It felt like a good opportunity to invite him to participate in a fatherly activity.

I asked him to take a look, and he agreed, following me outside to my seafoam green Accord. "Well, yeah, this needs four new tires. You probably need some wipers too—and an oil change," he said, his head under the hood.

To my surprise, he wrote me a $300 check for tires before we went our separate ways. I'd heard stories that he'd always been generous, oftentimes getting himself into financial trouble because he gave more than he had. But I was still disappointed and unsure how to navigate the awkward exchange with the bank teller when it bounced the next week as I tried to cash it. I didn't know how to mention it to Dad, so I never did. I was too excited about our budding relationship and knew it was fragile. I didn't want to upset the balance in our new dynamic. *How important were tires? My car was still getting me places.* That is, until I slid right off an exit ramp in the snow traveling home for Christmas later that year, landing in a ditch during a blizzard and requiring Mommy to drive two hours in the snow to come get me — once again proving herself as the reliable parent. But my dad had long disappeared by then.

We stayed in touch through the spring. Exchanging emails and phone calls, I'd even heard him say for the first time in my life that he was proud of me, ensuing a warm tingle of delight that traveled down my arms. For years, I saved a message on my flip phone from him saying he'd only been calling to hear my voice but that my voicemail had been enough, no need to call him back. He seemed excited about our relationship too. Over and over, he'd say in his thick southern drawl, "This is so coo-wel. Yeah, so cool."

In April, I went to a friend's house for the weekend who lived near campus. Before heading back on Sunday, I asked to check my email on her family's desktop computer, set up in the eat-in section of the kitchen. I saw my dad had written, and my heart fluttered as it always did when I heard from him.

Subject: Can't Function Sorry
Date: Sat, 24 Apr 2004 12:01:53

Hey Steph,
     We need to talk, or rather I need to talk. I thought about phone but knew I would just lock up......I've wrestled with this for some time.
    I'll start off right at heart of matter and work back. (1st) I...."Your Dad".... have failed in every arena of life...... Marriage, Husband, Father, Life and Career. I am 50 years old, tired, broken, and defeated.
     Your mother left filed for divorce and totally wrote me off and out, she made it clear that I was not to write...call.... visit....that as far

as she was concerned I was to cease to exist, so this is what I did. I have honored everything she set in motion. Now she did open up after there was money and a trust fund but truth is if there had not been a Trust fund she still would
not be giving me the time of day.

Now there is no way to put words to it, but this was the darkest time of my life.....I begged God to take me home, but He wouldn't, and the Lord has brought me to place where I have a certain degree of peace and Zen "IF" I leave the past totally buried. I tried to make contact, but the pain is unbearable, it's as if everything is relived and replayed. It's just better to consider me as if I've passed on and have ceased to exist in this life and we will have all of eternity to get to know each other in Heaven. I am just an all or nothing type person and the most important years of your life were taken away from me and it just all seems pointless now, you're better off just letting it go for now and we'll do this after we get to Heaven in Christ. I'm sorry I tried but I'm just too messed up inside and am not able to deal with the situation.... there is just too much pain and defeat and I have not been able to press through to victory and don't care anymore, I'm too old and too tired to try .... I'm sorry.
>>>>>>>>>>>>>

Please try to understand and forgive me if can.................Love Ya
Your Dad the looser

Words fail to describe the hairball of emotions that tangled inside me as I sat exposed in the kitchen to this nice, loving, andcomplete family I'd just met that weekend. I felt so sorry for my dad, I wanted to run after him before he slipped through my fingers again. I could see how tormented he was—haunted by a past that still controlled him.

I felt defensive of my mom, who, by my estimation, he deeply misunderstood—and why did it always have to be about his relationship to her? Their marriage was no more, but I was still his daughter, how could he shut me out so easily?

I also felt deeply rejected and embarrassed. We'd spent the past three months getting to know each other. His disappearance felt personal this time. At the funeral, he hadn't expected to meet me, it had been a surprise. This time, it was his idea to meet for lunch. His idea to stay in touch. And now his idea to retreat and go back into hiding.

I took a few deep breaths and tried to imagine where he was coming from. I could tell from the scattered way he'd written the email he was likely in a manic state. The quality of his spelling and grammar was always my first clue. I knew he was a wild card; I knew he struggled with mental illness—perhaps his brain chemistry was unbalanced. I just didn't know what it felt like to be a recipient of his chaos yet. *What was he asking for? What was he telling me?*

He needed space. It wasn't what I wanted, but it was clear it was what he needed.

I sat there, taking a deep breath in my friend's parents' kitchen, and I wrote him back. I told him if the best way I could love him was to stay quiet and give him space, then I would. But it was important to me that he knew, regardless of time apart, or what he had or hadn't done, I did love him. I said I would honor his request because I wanted to respect what he needed but mentioned he would always be my father—I only had one—and no matter what, I would always love him. Then, just as a reminder, I signed my letter:

Your Daughter,
Steph

Chapter 5
Chasing The Dream

After Guatemala, I was hungry for more experiences in the big, beautiful world. I wanted to pursue life beyond my bubble, so I immediately signed up for a semester abroad in Africa and spent three amazing months at the beginning of my junior year, studying and traveling through Mozambique, Swaziland, and South Africa.

I'd spent the summer before that semester abroad also falling in love with a boy. Simon was a blonde-haired musician on campus with notably plump, red lips. He was a year older than me, a senior. I loved his band, and the poems and songs he sent me privately. We'd written emails all summer while he was away as a camp counselor, and they continued when I was an ocean away, studying in Africa.

Arriving back in the States, I was an undeclared, second semester Junior, wasting money at a small private liberal arts college and living on a prayer that I would just… figure it out. I just knew I loved Simon and saw a future with him. Unexpectedly, a vision began to take shape when I went to watch him compete in a battle of the bands. The director of the competition was a friend and asked me to take the stage as a logistical favor, to fill a timeslot. I was happy for a chance to sing after a two-year hiatus and used my doe eyes of persuasion to convince Simon to accompany me. To both our surprise (and probably to his band's dismay), I won.

The grand prize of the competition was a short set on Main Stage at a music festival two weeks later. In the days leading up to the festival, I wrote songs, threw a band together — including Simon on guitar — and arranged a cover of MxPx's Invitation to Understanding. After letting music go, assumedly forever, and running away from it as far as across the world, here I was, trying again. Risking, and feeling alive doing it. I was quickly reminded of a deep knowing I'd been privy to for as long as I could remember; singing was a supernatural experience, a place where I easily found purpose and peace.

Two weeks later, on the Main Stage, I sung my heart out, singing from a place within that I had never accessed before. Two guys had made their way to side stage during my performance. They said they played with one of the bands performing later, so I handed them my demo CD, giddy they'd paid any attention to my set. It felt as though there was some energetic force, like a snowball rolling downhill, that was gaining momentum around me.

I made my way to catering behind the stage with the limited "artist" privileges that had been bestowed upon me, and as I beelined it for the buffet, someone stepped in my path. He was wearing a light pink T-shirt, a hat, and aviator sunglasses. Scruffy faced, he smiled and presented his hand to greet me, saying, "Excuse me, Stephanie? I'm Toby."

I froze, assuming it was a prank initiated by a friend who'd slipped some random dude $5 to pretend he was my childhood music idol, TobyMac (formerly one third of dcTalk, the band I had been obsessed with in high school). Calculating my next move, and not wanting to give my friends the pleasure of tricking me, I stared back at him silently. Suddenly, the countless hours of observing this man from afar collided with the reality that he was presently standing right in front of me and somehow knew who I was.

"OH MY GOSH—YOU ARE TOBY!" I said dramatically, abandoning all attempts to play it cool. "I am a HUGE fan!" I offered, with absolutely no chill.

"I heard," he smirked a boyish side grin. "I heard you start singing while I was having my coffee on the bus, and I sent my band out to watch your set. They said you crushed it out there and brought your demo back to the bus. I just listened to it, the production and song-writing needs some work, but I like your voice a lot. I wanted to meet you."

Four months later, Toby personally offered me a record deal with his label, Gotee Records. It felt like fate. Hands-down, there was no other label on earth I wanted to be part of. I was well aware of Gotee's cool, fringe status amongst Christian music culture, with artists like Jennifer Knapp, Sonic Flood, Out of Eden, Relient K, Family Force 5,

House of Heroes, and John Reuben—to name a few. These artists helped raise me, shape me, and inspire me. And now, I was one of them.

In my wildest dreams, I couldn't have imagined that this would be my real life. I drove into Nashville in my '93 green Honda Accord with stars in my eyes, two suitcases, a blender, and a toaster in my trunk, with no place to stay but the living room floor of a friend's apartment.

It was all coming together. Simon would move to Nashville while I figured out my senior year... Except that's not how it happened. Simon did move to Nashville and promptly broke up with me. I was devastated. So, I clung harder to my new record deal to provide the distraction and validation I was craving.

Around the same time that I was beginning my new life in Nashville, my mother moved from Pennsylvania to Indiana for a job. She had been a safe and steady landing place for me, but the tone of our relationship was shifting as she was seeking more and more support from her two constants: her children. The tension was, we were trying to launch, entering the workplace, and chasing our respective dreams in our early 20's, but she was desperately clinging to us as so much of the life she'd known was disappearing. She had left her community, her dying parents, and her job of 13 years, and moved across the country to a city by herself where she knew no one. She was hurting, lonely, and scared—tossed in the waves of her own change—but sadly, we didn't have what each other needed. As invincible as I wanted to believe I was in my early 20's, I still needed support myself as I also began a life and career in a new city of my own. As our relationship changed, so did the ways I looked for support.

I poured myself into writing and recording my first album. But I also made sure I always had a male suitor interested and in pursuit of me. Men helped silence my anxiety and fear. I didn't want to let a relationship distract me, so I never let anything get too serious, but in doing so, I obviously got distracted. It took so much energy to make sure someone was on the line, while trying to appear nonchalant about it all. I learned how to build armor around my heart, vowing I would always leave before being left. As long as I had my record deal, boys could come and go.

I worked part-time at Starbucks as to not burn through my signing advance. The dream was alive, within reach, and although I wondered why Toby wasn't more involved in the making of my freshman album, he would pop in from time to time, and I told myself to be grateful for whatever scraps of time he would throw my way. I didn't want to be a waste of time. I couldn't face the possibility I would let anyone down. I needed this album to prove to everyone, myself included, that I had something to offer.

The early 2000's were an interesting time for the music industry in general, as it transitioned with growing pains from CD-driven sales to the wild west of digital sales. I got tossed in the waves of that change. I had 5 A&R changes before I finished my first album, two and a half years after signing. Once it was done, I was anxious to release it and hit the road, but we had to pause the release for eight months because of a distribution change the label was navigating. I struggled to not interpret the label's irregularity and unpredictability as personal, rather than what it was: an attempt to navigate uncharted waters and keep the doors open. I felt like I was on the back burner, and I was, because quite frankly, they had bigger fish to fry.

Through the lens of my 21-year-old life experience, Toby's delay to responding to an email, and his lackadaisical participation in my first album, felt devastating. I deeply desired him to mentor me in this new chapter of life — the way he had for other artists before me. But it wasn't happening, and I understood it to mean the issue was me. Once again, it felt like I was being rejected, deemed unwanted and unimportant.

Of course, this had more to do with me than it did with Toby or the music industry. When I first walked through the doors at Gotee, I was freshly heartbroken over my breakup with Simon, it had only been one year since my father's second rejection of me, requesting I pretend he was dead, and I couldn't seem to find my once stable and strong Mommy — she'd been replaced by an insecure woman who cried every time I tried to end a phone call. I felt orphaned at a time when I still desperately wanted parents. It also had only been one short month since my Grandpa Ken died. Grandpa Ken, alongside Grandma Billie, helped raise me. He taught me to mow the lawn, he cuddled me on the couch while he watched baseball and I napped, and he sang harmony with the voice of an angel. In a way, he was the only dad I'd ever really known. My grief over my breakup, dad's rejection, the change in my relationship with my mother, and my grandpa's passing was still tender to the touch when I met Toby. So, it's fair to say my expectations of his role in my life were rather high.

When my presumptions of being a signed artist didn't align with reality, I began to struggle personally and spiritually. After several years on the label and a failure to launch the way we'd all expected, I wondered if God had forgotten me. Forgotten about the momentum and excitement I originally experienced in being "discovered." Initially, the excitement had been palpable. *Where had it gone? Had I done something wrong, gone off the rails somehow, and God was withholding to teach me a lesson? If so, what lesson?* I was trying my hardest to do everything "right."

In those early years of my adulthood, I was unable to see the impact my dad's silence and rejection had on my functioning in the world. I was not yet ready to look my desire for a man's attention in the eye, nor was I ready to explore the depths from which it was rooted. That felt too vulnerable, as though acknowledging that desire within me meant I was allowing my wounds to define me and show weakness. I didn't want to have a cliché "daddy wound," I wanted to be better than that; separate, superior, or immune to it somehow. I had no idea my insatiable desire to be seen and valued was actually a gift, attempting to ground me in reality and point me to the areas where I needed to heal the most.

My desire wasn't wrong, it was misplaced. We all have an innate desire to be special, but I mistakenly believed someone else had the power to confirm or deny that about me. I unconsciously "shopped around" for my belonging, specifically to men whom I assumed could deem me as worthy. Because I was afraid of my own hurting and hungry heart, I tried to outrun it, even silence it, rather than bring it — in all its need — to the One who had already established my value. Unfortunately, my inability to face my own pain allowed my pattern of chasing affection to continue, and I injured some good people in the process.

Once, in what I can now see as a very Fatherly moment, Toby gently mentioned something to me in a conversation (that I remember absolutely no context to because I was so mortified). His tone was kind, and playful, but slightly concerned as he said I was earning a reputation for myself as "Boy Crazy." In a very cool cat manor, he raised an eyebrow and gave me a chance to respond. I felt exposed, because I knew he was right, but instead of having any willingness to own it, my best thinking was to deflect and cover up with humor, responding that I couldn't help it if the boys saw something they liked, twirling my hair playfully. I assured him I was focused on music and I vowed to myself to not get distracted, or at least, to hide it better.

I wasn't motivated by sex or physical affection, although I enjoyed a good make-out as much as the next 20-something, but my insatiable desire was more that my soul needed to know I was valued, important, and worth pursuing. I couldn't get enough of it. I found myself acting almost compulsively, trying to catch a gentleman's eye, and wondering how long I could hold their gaze. Like a game, once the challenge had been won, I would move on to an exciting new person that caught my eye, subconsciously trying to prove to myself, my dad, and maybe even Gotee, that I was, in fact, desirable and of value.

Over time, I established such a pattern that I remember worrying I wouldn't be able to love just one person for a lifetime. I didn't understand how much of a vacuum I was, and how one-sided the love exchange was. I didn't understand that true intimacy would only be birthed through commitment itself. Instead, I danced from love interest to love interest, all the while using my career as a guise for why I couldn't stick around for too long.

I wish I could say I was more emotionally aware at the time, but I wasn't. I was still constructing my first draft at showing up in the world. It wouldn't be until later that I would begin to understand my part in the heartbreak of my own dream at Gotee not coming true. When I didn't get the validation I hoped for from my career, I started shopping for it elsewhere. I spent energy maintaining male attention that I could have spent discovering my own voice. I'd always sensed there was a song in me, but I didn't know how to find it. So, I avoided it.

I didn't understand that Toby's silence and distance was not personal because it felt personal—much like my father's. Had I known then that my feelings were not facts, I might have understood that Toby had a solo career he was building, an entire label to manage, and a family of his own he was caring for. He had in fact seen something special in me and generously handed me the opportunity to unlock it. It's as if he handed me the keys to a Ferrari, but I didn't know how to drive yet and I was too scared to find help. Instead of learning how to drive, I kept hoping for a ride.

The reality is, I have one hand that builds, and one hand that tears down. Eventually, I would learn to wrap both hands around myself and hold all the various parts of me, but much like a pattern cannot be broken and changed until it is first recognized, I would tear down until I learned to build.

Early in my career, I did an interview, sharing how my dad called me the wrong name when I first met him and how I'd chosen to forgive him. Overnight, it seemed, my "ministry" was born. Every event I sang at, I was asked to share my story and speak on the power of forgiveness. I was considered a role model for other kids whose dads abandoned them. As a result, sometimes I felt pressured to seem healed so I could be a good example and have a dramatic-yet-resolved story to tell. I didn't extend myself the luxury of seeing my story as one still in process. I didn't know how to hold the tension of all that was still unresolved in me with the lessons I was still learning. Instead, I only focused on the shiny parts and didn't look too closely in the shadowy corners of myself.

Before I knew it, I began to detach from my own experience because I didn't know how to be the little girl in that story, still processing and healing from my dad's rejection. Instead, I talked about the little girl as if she were someone else, and the story had a pleasant, pretty bow on it. But it didn't. It wasn't wrapped up at all. It was still unfolding… or unraveling.

***

I honored my dad's request in his breakup email for over two years, until I woke up from a dream about him one night in summer of 2006, shortly after moving to Tennessee. Although the details of the dream are fuzzy, I sensed an urgency to tell him that his life still had purpose and meaning. Sure, he'd asked me to pretend he was dead but in reality, he wasn't. He was still alive. And after this dream, I was willing to potentially offend him by making contact—I had to at least try.

I spent the day trying to talk myself out of it, but eventually constructed an email and hoped the address I had from two years ago was still good. It was a Monday night, just after Father's Day, and I pressed 'send' in a moment of bravery before closing my computer and going to bed. To my surprise, he responded in the wee hours of the morning. In his email back, he explained he'd recently gotten off the road trucking, sold his house, and gone back to school to get his architectural license updated. He'd gotten a job at a good firm, and all was well, until he freaked out on a Thursday afternoon and left a notice on his boss's desk, informing him that he quit. By Monday morning (the same morning I woke up from the dream), with no job and no direction for what was next, he was realizing what he'd done. With his savings drained and no employment to speak of, he was regretting his decision but couldn't find the courage to ask for his job back. Feeling like he'd messed up again, his fear compounded and intensified, accusing him that time was running out to get his life together. In his own words, he was contemplating "frying his bacon" until out of nowhere, he received an email from his estranged daughter whom years prior, he'd asked to pretend he was dead, saying that he still had purpose.

He said he was planning to visit Steve in Virginia to do some soul searching and mentioned that, after hearing from me, he thought it was time we see each other again. He asked if he could stop in Tennessee on his way to Virginia from Arkansas. I agreed, and within days, he was passing through town.

As I pulled into the Best Western to meet him, I saw him pacing the parking lot, filling empty spaces with his long, nervous strides. I smiled, endeared by his obvious anxiety over seeing me again, and waved as I parked next to the spot he was now standing in.

"Hi Dad!" I said cheerily as I got out of the car, attempting to put him at ease with my warmth.

"I can't believe you're still driving this thing!" he said, slapping the hood of my faithful-but-faltering '93 Accord, adding, "I'm gonna buy you a new car!" He delivered this greeting, foregoing a "hello," and although he said it with all sincerity, I felt the need to pull the reigns on his fervor.

"Whoa. Maybe let's see how dinner goes first," I said laughing, testing the waters of levity so as not to engage with another empty promise.

He seemed to notice his impulsiveness and laughed with me, agreeing we would stick to dinner and a movie for the evening. But by the time we met at Shoney's for breakfast the next morning, he had devised a plan. He was going to get a job trucking again. Then he could get approved for a loan and buy me a more reliable car. He felt like having that as a goal would be a good motivator for him to follow through on getting the job, some might even call it: purpose? He went on his way, and I didn't hear much from him until he called a few months later in a manic high. Out of breath, he told me he'd been approved for a loan, and I needed to go to the Acura dealer, talk to a salesman named Marty, and pick out whatever brand-new car on the lot I wanted. Dumbfounded, I pushed back. We had previously agreed on a reasonable used-car budget of $7,000-$10,000. I told him it was too much, and I didn't need a brand-new car, I hadn't asked for any of this, and I didn't want him to get in over his head. But he sobered up quickly and spoke to me clearly.

"Steph. I do not know how to be a father to you. Something in me is broken. But I do know how to take care of this one thing, I can buy you a car — the nicest car I can afford. You don't have to understand, I just need you to let me do it." Three days later, I was the owner of a new, black pearl, 2006 Acura TSX.

That was the third time my dad and I ever met, and he disappeared again after that. Without the shared goal of finding a car between us, contact with me once again proved to upset the small amount of balance he was able to find in isolation. Over the next several years, I would check in on him with a birthday greeting or a random *Hello*. Sometimes he responded, sometimes he didn't. I never pushed if he ghosted me, I only savored the times when he didn't. But he was never one to initiate contact.

I learned to take what I could get from him, and I drove that Acura for years, affectionately naming it "Hamilton" (my dad's middle name). Every time I sat in the driver's seat, I felt like he was giving me a hug, affirming my value with premium heated leather seats. It was the unspoken, unconventional love exchange we had agreed on.

***

A few years after saying goodbye at the Acura dealer and losing contact again, I was deep into my touring years, traveling the country in a van with my band. I noticed we were playing a show in Arkansas, and it was close to my dad's house. I impulsively decided to cold-call him on our way to the event, invite him to the show, and ask if my band and I could stay with him that night. He told me his place was small and he didn't have a bed in his guestroom, but I could sleep on the couch and he would buy the guys a hotel room.

To my utter delight, he came to the show that night at a festival in a rodeo arena. My band and I got on stage, did a quick line check, and gave the MC a thumbs up. I had eyes on my Dad in the audience, savoring this moment as it would be the first time he'd ever hear me perform.

The MC began, and instead of the usual "Toby Mac personally discovered this girl" intro I was used to, he started reading a bio on a piece of paper he'd printed off the internet.

"Let me tell you a little about this next artist," he starts. "When this young lady was only 14 years old, she met her father for the first time at a funeral. And he called her by the wrong name..."

I felt all the blood drop from my head, and I knew I had to intervene. I quickly ran to the MC, grabbing the mic from his hand.

"That's all true, my dad and I have a unique story. But I have some exciting news today, he is here — right now! This is his first time seeing me perform, everyone, let's make him feel welcome."

I gave the MC a look, clearly communicating my intro was over, and my band started the first song. Afterwards, I found my dad and brought him back to my greenroom.

He awkwardly tried to bring up the intro, "Man," he started with an exhale, "I don't know how you find words so quickly. You just jumped into action back there and spoke so fluently. I would've just frozen. I'm like a deer in headlights, and I just get tongue tied."

I could tell he was sincerely in awe of how I was able to improv and take control of the situation, and it felt like he was thanking me for not embarrassing him more, but my heart broke that he might have felt villainized in any way. It made me question if it was worth telling a few dramatic moments from our shared story to thousands of strangers when all I wanted was to move forward in building something new together. It was a sobering question to ponder, would I share my "testimony" the same way if the person involved in my story were standing in the audience?

I couldn't sleep that night on the couch. I heard Dad awake around 5am, shuffling about and eventually putting a sermon on in his bedroom. When I got up around 7am, I could smell that he had made a pot of coffee. I went into the kitchen to try and find a mug, and I opened cabinet after cabinet, but they were all empty. He had a few paper plates, a few canned foods, but mostly bare cabinets.

He came into the kitchen after hearing me move about and said, "I only have one mug, here, lemme wash this one for you." Then he added, "I hope I didn't wake you. I was so nervous about you being here, I woke up and have been vomiting since 5am."

My band picked me up about an hour later and I cried the whole way home. I couldn't pull it together. I'd seen a glimpse into his world, and it was so lonely and isolated, and my fear was that I'd furthered that on stage in a room full of people, when he'd showed so much courage to show up.

***

By 2009, after a string of relationships gone wrong, I began to see the wake of my own unhealthy emotional pattern. I'd come face to face with the impact it had on others after one particularly messy love-triangle breakup, and it broke my heart to see the pain I'd caused. It was clear this wasn't who I wanted to be. I knew I needed some help as I was finally ready to investigate some of the darker places within me.

I began seeing Al Andrews at Porter's Call in Franklin, Tennessee. Al served as a counselor, Spiritual Director, and guide of sorts to many artists in the greater Nashville area, and I am forever grateful for his wisdom, time, and resources.

After a summer of counseling and rebuilding my emotional buoyancy and boundaries—and no boys—my spirits were lifted with some good news that arrived with the changing colors of fall. I was hitting the road! Toby was putting together his own tour, Winter Wonder Slam. My band and I would finally be able to leave Nashville and sleep through the night, rather than driving through it. We had bus slots for the first time ever! And I was scheduled to perform right before Toby's co-headliner, Relient K.

The 20-city tour would span arenas across the country over the course of two months, ironically opening at the Bryce Jordan Center in my hometown, State College, Pennsylvania. It was a dream come true. I'd gone to concerts in that arena, had my high school graduation there, and spent many nights falling asleep fantasizing of playing on that stage. Now it was all happening, including the part where I was opening for my childhood idol! After three years on the label, it felt like I finally had some momentum again.

By the time the tour neared its end in December, we were in Sacramento, with only five shows left. Shortly before show start that evening, it was announced that there'd been a family emergency and the lead singer of Relient K, Matt Thiessen, needed to fly home to Ohio on a red eye after this evening's show.

I offered a courtesy "Let me know if I can help in any way — not sure what I can do, but I'm here if you need me!" as I made my exit from the meeting in the production office.

A few minutes later, my phone buzzed with a text from my honorary tour-big-brother, Ethan Luck, who also happened to be playing drums for Relient K at the time. "Can you come back?" he asked.

"Be right there," I responded, already in route.

The band had decided to stay and fly out the lead singer of another Gotee Band, House of Heroes (HOH), to finish the tour. The catch was, HOH was finishing their own tour across the country in Florida, and their lead singer, Tim, could only make the last three dates of the four remaining shows, still leaving one show without a lead singer for Relient K.

Ethan was the one who made the ask, "Steph, can you be the lead singer of Relient K for one show?"

Um. Hell yes!

All in all, we pulled it off! Fresno was gracious and the promoter asked me what he could buy me as a gift to thank me for saving the day. For some reason, I said I needed new pillowcases. He laughed, assuming I was joking, and asked me again what I wanted. I can still see his face when he realized I wasn't joking, I think he felt sorry for me. But I didn't feel like I had done them a favor. Instead, it felt like they had done me a favor. I didn't feel like I deserved to be on that stage, the imposter syndrome was still strong within me, and I was worried they'd all figure it out soon enough. After assisting in saving this man hundreds of thousands of dollars, I couldn't fathom asking for anything more than a pillowcase.

I knew of this Tim guy they were flying in to relieve me of my lead singer duties. I'd been a fan of his band (HOH) since college, and it was obvious they were the label darlings. He took a red eye from Orlando and landed in Las Vegas the same morning he would begin the three-show run as lead singer for Relient K. Apparently, on the short notice he was given, no one had mentioned, he was also expected to play guitar. He'd only learned the lyrics and melody on the plane, leaving rehearsal to knock out guitar parts. But he'd done it, of course. *(insert eye roll here) Who was this guy?*

Tim and I had rubbed shoulders in greenrooms and played some of the same music festivals, but he and his band were based out of Ohio, and I was in Nashville. I'd never had a complete conversation with him. I wondered if he was like some of the other band guys I'd met, a wanderer who never had to face the consequences of reckless behavior, moving from city to city, venue to venue, girl to girl.

The final show of the tour was in Phoenix. I had grown accustomed to Toby's standard of touring, which included a private mobile barista set up for the mornings. Zombie-like, I rolled out of my bunk, still sporting the T-shirt I'd slept in and some award-winning bleach-blonde-bed-head, as I waited for Danny, the traveling barista, to finish my Americano.

On this particular day, we were playing in the US Airways arena where the Phoenix Suns play. I could not have cared less, hence my first stop being the coffee bar, but all the band guys had heard rumors that the team was practicing, inciting an NBA player scavenger hunt.

As I waited for my go-go juice, I noticed Tim walking toward the coffee bar. He was still in his plaid pajama pants, falling a little short on him around the ankle, and his T-shirt looked smaller than mine as it revealed the slightest bit of his midriff. *I didn't know he wore glasses*, I thought to myself as I proceeded to judge that they were quite out-dated. He looks like an innocent little boy, I gathered. Watching him walk in my direction I felt my heart soften towards him. *Maybe he wasn't the asshole lead singer I'd pegged him for?*

He said my name warmly as he reached for me and pulled me into a full-on bear hug, nuzzling his face, ever so slightly, in my messy hair. I was surprised, he was quite disarming, and my heart betrayed my brain's cynical synopsis of him. *This is nice*, I mused, hugging him back, matching his measure of squeeze. After a few beats, I noticed he wasn't letting go. *Should I let go? But he's not, what do I do?* I tried to calculate my next move. *Is this nice, or weird?* Deciding it was sweet, I didn't want to be the one who broke the embrace, so I just settled into it.

Let's see where this goes, I thought, as he finally moved out of the embrace—just on the line of it getting weird.

Chapter 6
A Hero or Zero?

A few months after the Toby tour ended, Tim texted to let me know he was in Nashville working on music. He asked if I wanted to sing on the new House of Heroes record, *Suburba*. There was a song called "God Save The Foolish Kings" that had a *West Side Story* vibe, and they needed a female voice to be the Maria character. Everything was done but vocals, so the rest of the band had gone back to their families in Ohio, while Tim stayed behind to finish.

I agreed immediately, and as we figured out the logistics of when I'd come in to record, he added, "We should probably hang out first while I'm in town and all, it's way overdue." I almost dropped my iPhone 3G, I was so excited about both invitations! Before I could respond with something witty, another text came in: "Ya know, so you feel more comfortable in the studio and all ;)" Okay, there may or may not have been a winky-face included, either way, the message was received: he was interested and noncommittal, hook, line, and sinker for yours truly. Challenge accepted. I will make you want me.

Tim came over to my place the night before I was scheduled to sing in the studio. I was working one of my three jobs at the time and had to close the store that night. I raced home to freshen up and set some ground rules with my roommates before he got there.

Living in a condo with my two best (and very protective) friends, meant they wanted to vet — er, uh — meet the guy I'd been babbling about since getting home from tour. When I opened the door to welcome him in, I noticed he brought a backpack with him. Slung over one shoulder, he clutched it with one arm as he casually tucked a few fingers from his other hand in his front pocket. I got the sense he didn't go anywhere without it; it was a security blanket of sorts for him. I found it endearing and boyish. *Charming*. He stepped inside, and I immediately introduced him to Emily and Lindsey, my besties.

They stuck around for a little while, but eventually caught enough of my side eye cues that it was time to leave, retreating to their respective bedrooms for the evening and surrendering the living room to Tim and me.

It was so easy to talk to him. He was incredibly smart and gentle natured. He wasn't anything like the persona I'd seen on stage. We talked for nearly two hours, then—because we were in our 20's and invincible—decided midnight was the perfect time to watch a movie. I didn't want to suggest something dumb, so I made him pick through the shared roommate stash of DVDs—who knows what it was, I was just elated he was sharing a couch with me. Thinking back on it now, I have no recollection of what we watched, because I only remember what was going through my head. For some reason, I couldn't remember how to sit on a couch casually. *What were these limbs attached to my torso? And what was I supposed to do with them to look normal? Should I stretch out, sit closer, sit farther? Was I breathing too loud? Should I look at him? Did I laugh too hard at that part? What was he thinking?*

When we stopped directing our attention towards the TV, we talked some more, until eventually around the 3 a.m. mark, we agreed we needed to be able to sing the next day in the studio, so Tim made his exit. Hugging me again, much like in Phoenix, he lingered, arms wrapped around my core, only this time, it wasn't long enough.

I tried to go to sleep, but knew I was far too wound up. I was pumped about this guy. I turned on my light, pulled my journal from my nightstand, and began to write…

Okay, I'm gonna need my heart to stop beating so fast if I am going to get any sleep tonight. He is so sweet. He loves his family and seems so levelheaded. And he's smart, but mysterious. What goes on in that head of his? Not to mention how stinkin' cute he is! I already can't wait to see him tomorrow… or later today, I guess!

I closed my eyes, pen still in hand, and my breathing regulated as sleep began to feel more like a reality. Drifting off somewhere in between conscious states, I sensed Wisdom whisper. As her words floated over me, I shook the sleep from my eyes long enough to grab them by the tail and write them down.

Stephanie, you are worth noticing without a performance. You don't need bells and whistles to be loved. Let Tim notice you, don't demand he notice you. If you want to see where this goes, then respond to him, but don't initiate. You will need to know that he chooses you without coercing.

The words felt like a gift, something to give my attention to. *I'll give it more time tomorrow*, I mused groggily, I was too tired right now.

Wisdom's words became a mantra for me throughout the summer. You may respond, but don't initiate. Tim lit up my heart with curiosity and confused me, simultaneously. He'd flirt playfully with me both publicly and on social media, as well as privately in our texts or occasional phone calls, then he'd disappear on me for weeks at a time—sometimes suddenly, leaving a question unanswered mid-text conversation. I'd wonder if he'd lost interest, or if I had imagined it all? Where did he go when he disappeared? Granted, we lived in different states, and both toured regularly so our schedules couldn't be more different, but it still baffled me. We hadn't explicitly spoken about the chemistry between us, but there was certainly a science experiment in play, even others at the label noticed it.

In June, Tim told me he was in town for a friend's wedding and asked if he could take me to a show before he drove back home to Ohio. He offered to pick me up in his new Toyota Corolla, which had been a topic of many text threads between us. This sounded an awful lot like a date to me, and I understood it as permission to get my hopes up. He didn't give me much notice, but I was more than happy to rearrange my entire schedule to be available. I bought a new faux leather jacket on clearance and spent my entire lunch break chattering to my co-workers about how cute he was.

Arriving at my door again, this time sans-backpack, wearing a long sleeve black thermal, black jeans, and black vans, I devoured him with my eyes. His shaggy Beatles-esque hair looked freshly trimmed, and he smelled like clean laundry. Grabbing my new jacket, I couldn't help but think about how cute we were together.

At the show, he bought my drink, and we saw a few mutual friends at the bar. One commented privately to me how we made a great couple and my chest burned. *Maybe tonight would be the night we make it official?*

Being with him, I felt as though I'd been accepted into a club I hadn't been able to break into on my own. People loved him and his music. He was well respected and held in high esteem, both at the label and among friends. His band had a cult-like following and could sell out a venue to loyal fans, who adoringly recited every lyric and anticipated every guitar riff. But Tim was a quandary to me. Granted, I was learning there was more to him than I'd originally thought, but I still wasn't convinced that he wasn't a philanderer like so many other band guys I'd met, even though he hadn't as much as held my hand yet.

On the drive home, Tim mentioned he'd been at his friend's wedding with his ex-girlfriend. The bride and groom were mutual friends of theirs, and although they'd been broken up for a while, they were on friendly terms and had agreed to go to the wedding together. She had driven down with him from Ohio but flew home earlier that day.

Of course! No wonder he didn't mention he was in town. Realizing I was an afterthought, my arms went numb.

Perhaps noticing my deflating enthusiasm, Tim continued. "She isn't right for me. The older I get, the more I realize I've been dating the wrong kind of girl."

"What's the right kind of girl?" I asked, intentionally keeping my tone and expectations low.

"Someone who doesn't need me to fix them," Tim said thoughtfully. "Someone who's got at least some of their shit together — and who my family would like." He paused, before adding, "But mostly, someone who loves God."

I wondered if he was talking about me. I hoped he was. I knew I had a reputation as a "good girl" in our shared circle of friends, but for some reason it had always felt more like a judgement than a compliment. But it didn't feel like Tim was looking down his nose at me. Rather, for a moment, sitting in his new Corolla, I felt like maybe he actually saw me.

The evening ended and nothing more was said to clue me in on what was happening between us, or how he felt about me. But I clung to the breadcrumbs of hope that he'd dropped as he disappeared back to

Ohio and his separate life.

More often than not, when he fell silent for a period of a time, I would see something that reminded me of him. Whether it was an inside joke, a shared interest, a movie trailer, or a new song, I'd be tempted to reach out and use it as an innocent point of entry into a round of flirtation. Don't initiate, I'd remind myself, he knows how to get a hold of you. I'd keep a mental list of all the things I wanted to share with him, if he ever did emerge again, and without fail, my face would flush when I saw a text or notification pop up from him, feeling released to show him a little more of my sparkle, once again.

Naturally, I gave up on him a few times, swearing him off, as he toed the line of playing with my emotions, until he'd surface again, inspiring a little more patience from my fatiguing heart. But by August, we'd been playing this back-and-forth game for nearly eight months, and I knew I couldn't take much more. I'd been patient and had a sense that he might be worth the wait, but it was time to either let go or move forward — I wasn't going to wait forever.

Once again returning to my journal, I complained to private pages about my dilemma. As I wrote with my preferred Sharpie pen on carefully selected paper, I had an overwhelming sense that I would know, one way or another, by the end of the coming weekend if Tim and I were going to progress any further or not. I felt peaceful with either outcome, yes or no. I just wanted off the rollercoaster and welcomed some clarity.

In true Tim fashion, he had casually mentioned he might be coming to town for a few days. No guarantees, and I assumed I would know at the last minute if he did, in fact, decide to come. Dropping hints at his flakiness, I'd told him I was going to pencil him in but wouldn't hold my breath. I figured if he didn't come, that would be answer enough for me. However, to my surprise, the weekend found us together all day, every day.

I braced myself for him to leave without a DTR (defining the relationship), and asked myself: *What I would do in that case? Would I bring it up? Was I willing to tell him how I felt first?* In all my gathering of info on Tim, the resounding feedback from his best buddies was that he usually let girls do all the work. He was the attractive lead singer after all, so he always had available options. There was always some girl fighting for his attention; he didn't have to be the pursuer; he was the pursued. I knew how to subversively play that part, coy and cool, but I didn't want to this time. Something in me knew my invitation to growth was to believe I was worth noticing without a song and dance. Conversely, Tim's growth was to risk and go for what he wanted. I decided if he didn't bring it up, I wasn't going to either.

Finishing another movie that I don't remember (perhaps it had Brad Pitt in it?) on the night before he returned to Ohio, we let the credits roll as we sat closer to each other than any of our previous late-night screenings. Eventually the DVD returned to the home screen, and Tim seemed nervous as he positioned himself to face me on the couch we were sharing.

He monologued for a while, and I intuited that he was about to confess his affection for me, but I didn't want to get ahead of myself, so I listened with a poker face. He continued long enough that I second guessed my instincts for a moment, but eventually, he summarized with clarity.

"Steph. What I'm trying to say is: I like you. I like you a lot. And I like you for the right reasons. You don't need to be rescued, in fact, that's what scares me a little. I have a feeling the standard you require is going to challenge me, but I really want to see where this goes."

I took a second to savor the words I had been waiting so long to hear before releasing my poker face.

"I like you too!!!!!" I cooed, as he exhaled a nervous breath and swallowed me in a cuddle.

***

We dated long distance for eight months before Tim moved to Nashville in May of 2011. He lived with my good friend, Matt Olson, who had a room available. I was excited to merge our lives in a new way, finally exploring our relationship as residents of the same city.

But as delighted as I was to see more of him, I noticed I felt lonelier than when we'd lived in different cities. At least when we were six hours apart, I had a reason for the distance I felt between us. Now, I just felt like he was withholding from me. I experienced our relationship as surface level, and I wanted more. I also couldn't shake the feeling that he had some secrets. If we were really in this to see where it was going, I needed to know if he would open up and be willing to have difficult conversations with me.

We decided to take some space apart just two months after he moved to be closer to me. As he drove away from my condo that afternoon, I felt the temptation to panic and run after him, but I centered myself and practiced letting go. Although my impulse was to grovel, I didn't want to beg someone to love me deeply.

A few weeks later, we met for a walk at Radnor Lake. Tim told me about the space he'd taken and his renewed desire to grow with me. He told me about a camping trip he'd gone on with a friend and how he'd finally gotten honest about his fear of vulnerability and transparency. He also told me that he'd talked with his friend about an occasional porn habit and his desire to stop. His friend challenged him to surround himself with other people who were striving to live in a similar way, and upon

returning home, Tim had initiated a weekly meeting of the minds men's breakfast. I hardly recognized the person I was walking with. Even still, when he asked if I wanted to keep trying, it was a reserved "yes" I gave him. I absolutely still wanted to see where this went, I knew there was gold inside him, but I just didn't want to spend my whole life digging for it. Time would tell, and I was at least willing to give it more time.

In December, Tim and I drove to Columbus together in my Acura. Tim was a groomsman in his friend Nate's wedding on New Year's Eve. I dropped him off for the bridal party wedding festivities early in the day and entertained myself in the city for the afternoon.

On my way to the 7 p.m. wedding, flying solo in a city I was unfamiliar with, I glanced down at my GPS to confirm my upcoming exit. Glancing back to the road, I saw a mattress fall off the vehicle in front of me, just in time to hit it. The square mass of foam and springs lodged under my front two tires, and I lost control of my precious Hamilton. Swerving to the left, then the right, I danced across four lanes of interstate, until eventually, the mattress dislodged and left me stalled, a sitting duck, perpendicular in the fast two left lanes of the interstate. The Acura rebelled against my attempts to restart the engine, as I frantically turned the ignition key whispering "please, please, please," and monitored my surroundings, aware of my vulnerability to oncoming traffic.

Thankfully, the other drivers around me slowed, seeing what happened, and traffic was cautiously passing me in the open right two lanes of interstate. If I could just get Hamilton to start, I could move to safety and assess the damage. But he wasn't starting! I didn't know what to do, get out? Run across four lanes of interstate traffic? Abandon the one precious gift my dad had given me?

Keeping an eye on oncoming traffic, my momentary calm evaporated as I noticed a black sedan barreling toward me in the fast lane I was straddling. He doesn't see me, I thought as my attempts at the ignition became frantic. As the car approached at 70mph, my options quickly reduced to one: brace for impact.

A moment before impact, the driver of the sedan saw me, but it was too late. Cutting to the right in a last-ditch effort to avoid hitting me, he hit the nose of my car, sending my bumper flying and me spinning, disorienting me and dismembering my most prized possession.

Once I came to a complete stop, facing the concrete median dividing North and South I-71, I assessed my body for any injury. I had a bump on my knee, and I felt a little woozy, but I was miraculously unharmed. *I need to call 911*, I thought as I began to search amongst the wreckage for my phone.

Bzzz. Bzzz. A vibration buzzed at my foot near the gas pedal. I reached for it and saw that it was Tim, likely calling to check on my ETA for the wedding.

"Tim. Tim. Tim. Tim. Tim. Tim." I answered in my shock, unable to find words to explain what had happened only seconds before. I got stuck on his name, repeating it like a broken record.

"What's wrong? Steph, are you okay?" He asserted, knowing something was very wrong.

"I'm okay. But I was just in an accident. It's bad."

"Oh NO!! Are you okay? You're sure, you're not hurt? Have you called 911?"

"Not yet, I couldn't find my phone until you called. It just happened, like, now."

"Okay, you need to call 911. I'm going to find a car and get to you—"

"—No! You stay for the wedding, I am okay. I'm okay. I'll call 911 now."

I was grateful he offered to come, but the wedding was starting in ten minutes! I didn't want him to miss it, what could he do but wait for the tow truck with me? The thought then dawned on me that I was in a city I didn't know, I wasn't even sure where I was. I didn't know anyone here but Tim, I didn't even have his parent's phone number. "But will you call your parents and have them come?" I said, fighting off tears as I suddenly felt very alone. "And... just come when you can, once the service is over," I whispered before hanging up to call 911.

I waited on the side of the road in a cocktail dress and heels until Tim's parents arrived with a blanket and a warm car to sit in until the tow truck arrived.

As dusk turned dark, the tow truck's flashing lights blinked a hypnotic rhythm while the mechanic chained the symbol of my father's affection to his truck and dragged it onto the flatbed to be hauled away.

"You know why you're alive, right?" he said to me, leaning on the lever and trying to make small talk.

"Hmm, a miracle?" I said, not sure if it was a trick question.

"This car right here" he said, slapping the back bumper on Hamilton. "I tow cars all day, e'ry day, and more people walk away from Acura's than any other. Yup. This car rite here saved yer life young lady."

A flash of gratitude for my dad's insistence on buying me something beyond his means washed over me, but I instinctively clung harder to this token of his affection because we hadn't spoken in years. I didn't have a relationship to fall back on if this symbol was ripped away from me, this was all I had of my dad. I couldn't accept that it might not be salvageable. It had to be. I couldn't lose him again.

Just then, I noticed another set of lights coming toward me. Driving the wrong way in the right median was Tim. He'd asked a fellow groomsman for his keys as soon as the bride and groom kissed, then he'd left without telling a soul. He got out of the "stolen" Honda Civic in the median and ran to me, burying his head in my hair.

Tearing up he whispered, "I could've lost you—I never want to lose you," and kissed me on the side of the interstate.

Once Hamilton was towed away, Tim and I returned to the wedding for the reception and counted down to midnight, ringing in the new year together. I bummed some Advil from a stranger at our table for the stiffening of whiplash that was beginning in my neck, but I welcomed an open bar to calm my frayed nerves. Although it was a nice momentary distraction, later that night, the reality of what had happened began to sink in. Every time I closed my eyes, all I could see was the black sedan speeding toward me at 70 mph. Tim held me close and rubbed my back, neither of us saying much.
Circling back to the comment he'd made on the side of the road, Tim eventually broke the silence. "Steph, tonight I realized I don't want to imagine a life without you. I want to build a life with you. If it's okay with you, I'd like to start saving for a ring."

If it's okay with me? Are you kidding? It's about time! I savored the openness I was feeling from him.

"Of course, I'd love that."

Chapter 7
Marriage

By the next summer, Tim proposed at Grandma Billie's dining room table in Pennsylvania. Mommy was in on the surprise and helped him plan after he'd asked for her blessing. I knew I wanted to marry him, but I was also terrified of a lifelong commitment. There was a war inside me, afraid to enter marriage and equally afraid not to. I'd watched my mother struggle as a divorced single parent my whole life, and I didn't think I could handle that reality, if it ever were to become my story too. So, I resolved that if I was going to do this marriage thing, I would make it work at any cost.

A few days after our engagement, we decided to call my dad to share the news. Tim wanted to introduce himself over the phone, and I could tell my dad liked his gentle and steady demeanor right away. We invited him to the wedding, promising a formal invitation in the mail once our plans solidified, and with enthusiasm, he said he would come.

In the weeks leading up to the big day, I tried to balance my hope that my dad would make good on his promise to be there for me, with also trying to imagine what an intimidating circumstance it would be for him to enter. He didn't know my
mom had recently remarried, and I didn't want him to be blindsided at the wedding. I asked her to please tell him beforehand, so he could have enough time to digest the information. I felt like that conversation was between them anyway, and even though I was 28, I wanted to be the child in this dynamic. Plus, this was supposed to be my day, and I just wanted both of my parents at my wedding. Although their history was complicated, I hoped they could put their tension aside for one evening and show up for me.

But Mommy wouldn't contact him. She didn't want to deal with his (likely) venomous response. I empathized with her perspective, but suggested she block his email after she sent hers or even make a new email for this one exchange. She refused. We raised our voices, sitting in a parked car after a breakfast together, hoping the other would understand our individual and unique pain centered around this man. She had her reasons, and I had mine. I knew hers were warranted, but her refusal to understand mine deeply hurt me. She'd contacted him in the past, why was this the hill she was suddenly willing to die on?

At first, she said she didn't want to contact him because she had already been the recipient of enough of his wrath — fair — but eventually she told me she was hurt that I even wanted him there at all. That felt the truest. She was feeling the injustice of having to share my day with a man who hadn't chosen to share my life. She had poured blood, sweat, and tears into raising me, why should she have to share my wedding with a man who continued to abandon me? I could see where she was coming from, but I still wanted a permission slip for just one day, to have both of my parents in a room together on my behalf. Eventually, we agreed that while she wouldn't reach out to him, his invitation still stood.

Mental illness is a complicated thing within a family, and its effects are as diverse as the individuals impacted. Mommy and Matt have always struggled to understand the soft spot I have for my dad. It's hard for me to understand too, but it's always been there. In this instance, I refused to blindside him upon arrival, so I wrote him an email three weeks before the wedding to touch base, knowing he was likely to shoot the messenger. Even still, I would rather be the one receiving the fallout of his hurt, resulting in his seat sitting vacant at my wedding, than withhold information from him to manipulate the outcome I wanted. In my email, I let him know he was welcome, and I hoped he'd come. I mentioned that my Aunt Donna (who he knew from years before) had offered to sit with him so he wasn't alone at the ceremony or reception. And I made sure he understood that Matt (his son whom he'd only met and spoken with once) would be there. Finally, I informed him that Mommy had remarried and my stepdad, Doug, would also be in attendance.

Ten days before the wedding I received a response from him. Opening his email, I saw its length and grammar and knew it wasn't in my own mental health's best interest to read it. I asked Tim to read it for me and to give me the cliff notes. My dad wasn't coming, and he still believed my mom needed to come back to him.

Despite my disappointment, Tim and I had one of the most fun weddings I've ever been to. It was very DIY, I crafted my thrifty little heart out and called in every favor I could, and the result was a magical night. We threw together the most incredible wedding band for our reception and asked all our talented friends to take turns singing songs we'd picked out. At the end of the night, I sang "At Last" to Tim, and he answered by crooning "Something" by the Beatles to me. As a finale, we finished with a duet of "Nothings Gonna Stop Us Now" by Jefferson Starship, inciting an epic dance party sing-along with all our friends.

During the ceremony, my pastor at the time, Jamie George, stood at the altar with us and offered wisdom and insight that would shape us in the future, although it would still be a few years into marriage before we would dive into our own discovery of what he meant. "Tim, this woman does not sip life, she gulps it. She will challenge you to move. And Stephanie, this man is calm and constant, he will steady you, but also challenge you to slow down. Do not blow out your individual candles after lighting the marriage candle, but keep them lit, alongside and within the new union and commitment you make today. Your marriage will flourish if you do not lose yourself in it."

Our road to the altar had been a little bumpy, but we were hopeful optimists standing before each other, making vows before God, friends, and family in November 2012. Were we ready for such a commitment? Who can say if one is ever fully ready to dramatically change their life? You don't know what it's like to be married to a specific person until you're married to them. In other words, you don't know what you don't know.

Whether it be Disney, Hollywood, or the westernized church that shaped my expectation—I was convinced that my husband would shower me with affection, pursue me to no end, and certainly not be able to keep it in his pants once we said our "I do's." Honestly, I looked forward to this picture being painted for me. I was sub-consciously terrified that I wasn't wanted—stemming back to my surprise and unwanted conception, followed by my father's silence and lack of pursuit of me—and I desperately hoped my husband would silence those fears and single-handedly redeem all the broken parts of me. Obviously, I didn't have words for this as a 28-year-old entering the covenant of marriage, but I most definitely carried those subtle and unnamed hopes and expectations right over that altar with me.

What I didn't know, and what isn't advertised, is that marriage would press every button I had, exposing my deepest fears and insecurities, inviting me to repeatedly look at them (as opposed to avoid them or live in unawareness of them), until ultimately, learning how to grow beyond them, into a freer and more complete version of myself. Relationship, namely marriage, invites us to go to places within ourselves that we wouldn't dare venture on our own. The gift isn't that someone rescues you, but that they help reveal the areas you didn't even know needed healing... often by exposing our ego.

We all have an ego version of ourselves, some call it the false self. The ego wants to be significant, central, and important by itself, apart from anybody else. It wants to be both separate and superior. It is defended and self-protective by nature and considers any critique a personal threat. The ego is usually the representative version of ourselves we send out into the world, a "best version" that masks our struggles and shortcomings. It hates to be exposed, but it must be for personal growth because it is too fragile a foundation to build on. As Richard Rohr puts it, "The shadow self is not of itself evil; it just allows you to do evil without recognizing it as evil... We cannot really get rid of the shadow; we can only expose its game—which is, in great part, to get rid of its effects."[1]

Part of the mystery of marriage is the commitment to the process. Tim and I would make a valiant effort at constructing something with our shadow selves, but it would inevitably fail us, because it was meant to. And in doing so, we would be invited to find our true selves.

Just like we all construct an ego, we all have a true self. It has always been there—it is the spark of the Divine, a unique expression of love conveyed within each of us that connects us to a larger whole. The true self cannot be lost, but it does get buried by our ego self, and it is possible to forget, or never discover, who we truly are. But life will continually present us with opportunities to become aware of our ego self and to awaken to our true self.

Even still, as lovely of a sentiment as that is, the process of ego killing is not for the faint of heart. Something must live before it can die. Something must be built before it can collapse. It seems transformation isn't found in getting it right on the first try, but in surrendering to the burning of our first drafts, keeping what survives and applying what we learned as a result. After all, we can only trade our ashes for beauty if something has first burned.

Tim had lived most of his life believing that he was uniquely broken, stemming from abuse in his childhood. He believed if anyone actually knew him, they wouldn't possibly be able to love him. I was convinced I could prove him wrong if I just loved him hard enough, and sincerely believed I could single-handedly uproot his deep-seeded and pre-me-existing belief. Perfect fit, right? I didn't yet know that belief is a personal responsibility, and no one can believe enough for another person to experience transformation. Nor did I know just how deep rooted these beliefs were for Tim. How could I? I couldn't know him if he didn't want to be known.

In his experience, it was too risky to be truly known, so he sent his "Nice Guy Tim" representative-self out into the world instead. "Nice Guy Tim" was pleasant, funny, and easygoing. He didn't ask much of others, in hopes of not being asked for much in return. He knew how to get along with everyone; how to be badass enough to roll with the rebels, yet good enough to be a role model to the renegades. Mostly, he knew how to keep people at arm's length, and did he ever know how to keep a secret.

Interestingly, and likely not coincidentally, Tim married someone who wouldn't settle for his representative. After three years of marriage, "Nice Guy Tim" had left me lonely and disappointed. The trail of breadcrumbs to his authentic self had only awakened my appetite for the whole meal. As many of us do, I had married the potential I saw in him. I'd caught glimpses of his true self and I wanted more, but I didn't know how to find it.

***

Eventually, I felt like I was suffocating. In many ways, even after three years of marriage and nearly five years together, I felt like I was still earning Tim's trust, proving myself as an ally. *What would it take?* I wondered. I'd been invited into the first tier of his inner circle, but I couldn't seem to break through any further.

My own ego was agitated by how I had "played by the rules" and done things "right," but wasn't receiving the payoff I assumed I deserved. I hadn't slept with Tim before we got married, I had been to counseling to work on some of my issues, and I couldn't understand why things didn't seem to be adding up for me. I wanted a reward for being "good." But my understanding of "good" would first have to fail me. I couldn't see my own impaired beliefs about myself that I'd brought into our marriage. I just wanted someone to love me enough that I would believe I was lovable! I'd spent my life outsourcing the investigation, hinging the results on how others treated me, rather than doing the brave work of believing what was already true.

My father hadn't provided great results for the "you are wanted" category, and neither had my experience in the music industry. After six years on the label, I'd found myself sitting in the offices of Gotee and signing legal jargon, through heartbroken tears, terminating my record deal just months after becoming a wife. My confidence had eroded and the fear that I had been signed on accident haunted me. We hadn't been able to find a path forward together, and I couldn't deny any longer that it was time to leave the label, so I asked to be released.

To their credit, Joey Elwood, the gentle, wise, and gracious president of Gotee offered to gift me my masters as I left. In my humiliation, I took them and hid them away. In reality, it was an unheard of and generous gift, but in my shame, it was further rejection—as if to say, "We don't want these either, we are erasing you from our catalogue." I never shopped them around to other labels or re-posted them on any streaming platform. I just tried to disappear into my marriage— so much so that I legally dropped "Smith" from my name altogether. I didn't want to be Stephanie Smith anymore; in my understanding she was a failure. I would try again as Stephanie Skipper.

But the information I was gathering in my three-year marriage was Tim didn't want me either. He rarely made advancements sexually, I almost always initiated sex. Sometimes I would intentionally hold off to see how long it would take him, and weeks would go by. Knowing his sexual past was more colorful than mine, I was left to assume it was me he didn't want, not sex. He also resisted my attempts to connect with him emotionally, accusing me of wanting too much and sarcastically reminding me that food, water, and shelter were all he really needed.

Maybe I do expect too much, I'd rationalize, trying to excuse him, in hopes that my biggest fear wasn't true. *He married me, so he must love me. Just be grateful for what you have.* I'd muster some grace and try harder to accept him as he was, until my love-blood-sugar inevitably crashed again, ensuing another mousey request for a few more breadcrumbs from him emotionally.

We'd formed a small independent band together called Copperlily shortly after getting married, and by 2015, we made the leap to touring full time in coffee shops, bars, theaters, and living rooms. I found myself surviving off the connection we had on stage because we presented as cute, happy, and cleverly self-aware. But at home, I couldn't find my husband.

Sometimes Tim would deflect my requests for more, telling me that he couldn't read my mind. Other times, he would privately re-assign meaning to my words, moving the goal post to excuse his half efforts. But it never sat well with me, in fact, it was chaos. As time went on, I had more and more experiences of clearly asking for follow-through or intentionality from him, explaining that those things helped me feel safe and cared for in a relationship, only to be left wanting. I knew I had been generous to give him both hints and blatant requests for more. I set the bar very low, needing the win more than he did as my worthiness seemed to hinge on it. Just call when you say you're going to or be home when you say you'll be. I wasn't asking for too much, was I? If someone said, "Shoot for the moon," I may have thrown a "take me out to dinner once in a while" out as a Hail Mary.

I had an eroding vision of "together forever;" in our current state, it sounded like prison to my dying heart. When my best attempts to coach us through our miscommunications continued to fail, I pleaded with Tim to go to marriage counseling with me. To be clear, what I said to him was, "I feel like someone tied a cinder block to my ankles and threw me in the ocean." What can I say? Subtle wasn't working. I needed him to know I was serious, and to his credit, he was willing. We found a therapist and started doing a little work to try and find each other.

After about six months, I felt like we'd made some good progress—remember, the bar was quite low, so any sort of movement beyond our stagnant trajectory felt like a win—and I decided to commemorate our growth by permanently marking my body with a tattoo of Tim's handwriting. He had bought me a tattoo gift certificate for my birthday the year before, but I had been too indecisive to redeem it. I figured that a tattoo might be a great way to honor our progress and hard work, so I had Tim write down "To know. To Be Known." on a piece of scratch paper three times, and I picked my favorite of the three, booking the appointment for the week of my 32nd birthday.

Two weeks after my tattoo virginity was taken, while the ink was literally still drying in my melanin, the bottom fell out from beneath me. On a twelve-hour drive home from a string of shows in Pennsylvania, I asked Tim a question I'd asked many times before. Knowing he was a man living in the digital age, I asked how he was doing with porn. He'd been honest about his struggle with it while we were dating, but I hadn't heard much from him on the subject since we'd been married. We'd agreed that I could ask anytime, but it was his responsibility to let me know if he ever slipped up. I never asked if I wasn't in a place to extend a generous amount of grace and love if what I learned was disappointing, but I expected his answer to be like what it had been for the past three years of marriage, "It's a struggle, but I'm doing okay with it."

This time, instead of his generic response, he paused, gripping the steering wheel while his cheeks flushed and asked me a question in return, "Have I ever told you about the first time I was introduced to porn?"

"Yes," I answered cautiously, noticing his deflection, and obvious avoidance of my question. He continued with the story I already knew, how he'd been introduced to porn at twelve years old by a family friend, who also became his abuser. Tim had thrown up that night after seeing the film, upset and yet curious about what he'd seen. He'd been conflicted whether to tell his mom the next day, confused by both his loyalty to his abuser's request that he keep it secret, and his upbringing to respect adults, ultimately deciding to keep it a secret and privately struggling with porn ever since.

Yes, yes. I knew this. I tried to hold his story with care, letting him finish without interrupting, even though I was surprised he was acting like I didn't know this information already.

When it felt appropriate, I asked my question again. "I know all that, and that's part of the reason I've tried to be really gracious. But I am curious how you've been doing since we got married?"

"It's a struggle, I'm not saying it's easy. But I'm doing okay with it." There it was. The answer I'd heard so many times. But after the unexpected monologue about his introduction to porn, I couldn't help but feel like he was wiggling out of the question with a now stale response. I decided to seek clarity one more time and rephrase my question.

"I just want to make sure I'm understanding you correctly." I turned in the passenger seat to face him, carefully choosing to keep my tone gentle as if coaxing a scared animal out of hiding. Growing annoyed and defensive that I wasn't accepting his first answer by dropping the subject, he threw an "Okay…" my way, and I noticed his jaw tighten. I knew he was ready to move on, but I wanted the truth, and had a growing sense he hadn't given it to me yet.

"My understanding is that if you mess up, you will let me know. I haven't heard anything from you to believe otherwise, and I've asked every couple of months for three years now. The answer has always been the same. So, am I correct to understand that the last time you looked at porn was before we were married?"

There was a long silence, and I knew what was coming. I watched Tim's face drain of color, as his breathing intensified.

"No, that's not the case."

Chapter 8
A Fist Fight with Reality

I emailed Chris, the therapist we'd been seeing, the next morning as we drove home, imprisoned in the car with each other for another six hours after stopping for the night at Tim's parents' house in Columbus. We'd been gentle with each other so far, both having some tears, as Tim told me he'd slipped up a handful of times over the past three years. After I pushed for clarity, he'd offered the number "four or five" times in total.

By the time we were sitting in the offices of Sage Hill the following day for an SOS appointment, that number grew from "a handful" to "too many times to count," and it was becoming clear there was a lot I didn't know about this man. In fact, over the course of the next three weeks, Tim would slowly, like drips from a leaky faucet, disclose more pieces of a very incomplete picture that was beginning to come into focus.

As I would get my footing on the "new" reality I was living in, coaching myself that we could make it through even this, another sliver of information would surface and turn my world into chaos again. Eventually, I wasn't sure what was up or down, what was real or what was a lie. Why couldn't he just tell the truth? Would I ever find the bottom? I couldn't seem to find
my footing.

Was it just porn?
Were there other women?
How many people were you with before me? …Wait, that is not the same number you told me before we got married.

I felt like a fool. This was the second time I'd been blindsided by this man's sexual secrets. The first time, our relationship suffered a near-fatal blow over our very first Christmas together. We'd been dating for only four months when I drove to Columbus to be with him and his family for a few days, and to see House of Heroes play a hometown show.

The day after Christmas, Tim told me that he loved me. I felt like I'd just burst through the earth's atmosphere. I felt honored, special, and chosen hearing those words initiated by him. It was easy for me to say it back to him, as I devoured my perceived victory over winning his heart.

The next day, his band was rehearsing, and I tagged along to hang out with Colin's wife, Michelle, and their three kids, while the band practiced in the basement. Colin and Michelle had married young, and Michelle had been a band wife since the beginning. Well versed in the highs and lows of all things House of Heroes, she'd known Tim a long time, and assured me everyone was very excited about us dating.

I was glad to hear it and spilled the tea that Tim had just confessed his love the night before. Michelle squealed, enjoying our "girl talk" as she wrangled her squirmy toddler on the living room floor. Changing a diaper, she nervously asked if Tim and I had breached the subject of our 'history' yet.

I thought it was an interesting question, but more so, an interesting tone that she'd chosen. I assumed she was nervous to ask if I knew about his messy history with an ex. I did. A few weeks after we'd begun dating, Tim had asked if I was a virgin, and I'd answered yes. I didn't press him for an answer to his own question. I'd just joined him in the silence that followed my answer, until he whispered, "I wish I was." I'd cuddled him a little harder and told him it was okay. He hadn't offered any more. After a long pause, I submitted a guess in hope of learning more. I asked if it was with his most recent ex?

"Yes," he'd responded, adding, "there's more to it though. After we broke up the first time, she called two weeks later and told me she was pregnant. I don't know for sure if she was, I don't even know if she went to the doctor. She told me she miscarried shortly after, but I had already gotten a job the next day, I'd told the band, and I was preparing to tell my family. It may have been a lie, but I believed her at the time, and it kind of messed me up." He still wouldn't look at me, but he let me know he was done talking and seemed to brace for impact as he added, "I wanted you to know." I was so grateful he'd told me. I wasn't afraid of complicated; I was afraid of secrets.

Knowing Tim had shared all of that with the band, I answered Michelle's question about our 'history.' "Yeah, he told me about the possible pregnancy and general tumultuous history with his ex," confident we were talking about the same thing.

"Oh good! I'm so glad y'all have talked about it all," she said, seeming relieved. Still dividing her attention between me and a poopy diaper, she began to speak candidly and continued, "I remember the first girl it happened with—he was so sweet—he told his parents and the band and…" My ears rang and my stomach fell through the couch I was sitting on. First girl… meaning, there were more? When I realized Michelle was still talking, I forced myself to retain some of the information she was casually offering as she assumed it was shared or common knowledge. But it wasn't. Somehow, Tim had failed to mention any of this over the past three months.

Because of her multi-tasking, she didn't notice my silence or look up to see my pale face as she continued listing names of Tim's multiple sexual partners throughout the years.

Clearly, my poker face needed work because Michelle stopped mid-sentence and asked, "Uh oh. How much of that didn't you know?"

"All of it," I whispered.

I kept my cool until Tim and I were alone in the band van, then I became a puddle of emotions. I felt foolish that everyone seemed to know more about his past than I did.

Chaos lives between the story we tell and reality. Although I was hurt to learn the truth about Tim's past, I was devastated to not experience the gift of Tim offering it to me himself. It wasn't as much about what he had done, but rather that he had created chaos for me by offering a version of the truth that was not congruent with reality.

I was surprised that I suddenly felt rejected because we hadn't had sex yet, even though we had agreed to wait until marriage. I begged him to tell me anything else I might not know about him, but doubt grew inside me like a cancer. I had stumbled upon the truth; he hadn't offered it to me. I ached for him to comfort me, but he didn't know how. He was frozen in his own shame, and I watched him retreat within himself, leaving me lonelier than I ever knew was possible.

Because he was living with his parents at the time, and I was visiting from out of town, I couldn't find the composure to go inside. I didn't trust myself to maintain a facade and "play house" in front of them. So, after hashing it out in the band van longer than was beneficial, I jumped into my own car and drove to a Panera close by to sort through my feelings. I considered leaving without saying goodbye. But after interrogating my motive, it was clear I only wanted to leave so he would chase after me. It was obvious he was in no state to do that, and I would be sorely disappointed. Of course, I wanted the fairytale narrative of boy-loses-girl, boy-fights-to-get-girl-back, but I knew if Tim wanted to fight for this, he needed a different opportunity to do so.

Eventually, I calmed down enough to re-enter and stay for the rest of my planned trip. I knew Tim was feeling a betrayal of his own, as someone had shared intimate parts of his life without his permission. I'd noticed how young he appeared when he felt exposed, and my heart softened toward him. He looked like a hurt little boy in a grown man's body. It was obvious to me that he had some work to do in his own heart and soul, but I didn't want to add any evidence to the lie he already seemed to believe. The lie that if someone actually knew him, they would run away. I also wanted to believe people can change, that he could learn to tell the truth. I didn't want to be too judgmental, maybe he just needed more time to trust me? After all, we'd only been dating for a few months.

Eventually, we stumbled our way into the future because I was committed to knowing him, even if what I learned was painful sometimes. I believed he was worth it.

But I did live with an ambient fear that I still didn't know the whole truth. And as it turns out, that was the case. Here I was, years later, discovering the truth was hidden so deeply inside Tim, and I felt like I couldn't find the bottom of his secrets.

***

As Tim confessed the number of sexual partners was more than I'd known, the waters also muddied on the timeline of those ten months leading up to our official dating when we'd talked, flirted, and hung out. Although there hadn't been an exclusive commitment on "us," I had no idea he had been sleeping with multiple other girls during that time, all the while not even kissing me on dates. It was beginning to make sense why he'd been so slow to commit, why he had disappeared for weeks at a time, confusing me. He knew I wasn't a casual hook-up kind of girl and a relationship with me would require a halt to his philandering ways. But what I didn't understand was: why had he chosen me at all? Clearly, he didn't want me.

Like a mad woman, I found an old phone of his in his bedside table drawer and read recent flirtatious texts with girls I didn't know—one of which had a thread predating our marriage and she was begging him to not buy me an engagement ring. It seemed he was towing a line, flirting with the idea of cheating after white knuckling mono-gamy for three years. When I confronted him, he swore he hadn't broken any physical boundaries since we'd been married. But how long could he keep it up? Was I supposed to consider myself "lucky" to find out he was only texting with those girls, that nothing happened that one time, because she fell asleep before they could finalize any plans? More questions surfaced as I struggled to figure out what was true about our shared history and his personal one.

You had a recreational hook-up buddy for years? You had sex with a mutual friend of ours, and then took me to her house for a party once we started dating? Did everyone there know but me? You slept with your ex-girlfriend the same weekend you were in town for that wedding and took me on a date? Did I need to get tested for STIs?

I was now learning a whole other side of the person I'd paired my life with. As the truth came to light, my world fell apart. As stories changed, and reality shifted, I battled panic attacks, struggling to breathe as I repeated, "What am I gonna do? What do we do? I don't know what to do," like a broken record. The only thing that felt true was my biggest fear: I was unwanted. I'd been an unwanted surprise to my parents, my dad didn't want a relationship with me, the music industry didn't want me, and now, it seemed my own husband didn't want me. How could I interpret it any other way? The evidence was there, the jury had deliberated, the verdict was in, unwanted. Case closed.

I tried to believe our marriage counselor when he looked me in the eye and told me Tim's addiction had nothing to do with me, I'd heard that before — I probably would've told a friend that and meant it — but how could that be true? He clearly had a sex drive; it just wasn't directed at me. I hated my body, maybe this wouldn't be happening if it was just smaller, skinnier, sexier. I was convinced that Tim wanted a petite girl. He'd dated tiny girls in the past, his mom was tiny, his sister was tiny, it had to be that his standard of beauty was "tiny," so why had he married me? I knew his family thought I was a great choice for him, so had he just felt pressure to marry me? Was I the "safe" choice? Had he approached the age of thirty and felt the clock running out, so he settled for "marriage material" but he wasn't *really* attracted to me?

I also hated that word: addiction. I was scared of it. Our therapist, upon gathering the new information Tim had disclosed, suggested he go to 90 meetings in 90 days. He also suggested in-patient treatment at a three-month facility that would run us a bill of approximately $50,000. I already felt like this was costing me more than I could afford emotionally, what were we going to do? Plus, we'd just bought our first house, rubbing every penny of our self-employed musician income together to scrounge up the down payment. Our full-time job at the time was touring bars, coffee shops, living rooms, and churches in our hatchback, singing cute, happy love songs together as a duo. Now, it was all falling apart in front of me. Was I going to lose my house? My marriage? My career... again?

I was in triage. It was all unraveling so rapidly. Our trust was broken — and I still didn't know to what extent. But my goal was to stop the bleeding and get to a place where I could assess the damage. Desperate for another option, we visited an old friend and guide, Al Andrews at Porter's Call. On his recommendation, Tim reached out to a facility called Onsite to inquire about something called the Men's Healthy Sexuality and Intimacy Program. Al explained it to be a week-long workshop offering a unique therapeutic experience for men who were coping with unresolved past events through unhealthy sexual addictions and patterns. He told us a friend of his had developed the program and although our therapist's $50,000 suggestion may be a 'first class' seat to recovery, this was a 'coach' option—with maybe not as much legroom—but it could still get us where we wanted to go. He felt strongly that Onsite would be a safe space for healing, a first step in moving from shame and isolation into greater intimacy and connection for Tim.

It felt clear that was our next move, and we left Al's office with a sliver of hope. But we were still scared and didn't know how we were going to make it all work. Maybe it wasn't 'sell the house' expensive, but it was still 'drain the savings' kind of money for us.

Tim learned there was a program scheduled to begin in two days, but the woman on the other end of the line apologized at his inquiry to join; apparently, they were booked solid for months.

But we need help NOW! I thought as he recounted his conversation to me after hanging up, then told me he was going for a walk.

I didn't panic, something flickered inside of me, unwavering and steady. I knew Tim would be at that workshop in two days. Perhaps I was unwilling to accept a "No," or maybe it was my intuition, but I just knew he'd be there. I didn't know how we were going to pay for it, but I was sensing a growing invitation to trust, as a path forward seemed to be appearing.

Fifteen minutes later, the kind woman who had spoken with Tim called back and told him there had been a sudden cancellation, and if we could have $5,000 to them by 5 p.m.—which was in three hours— he was in. We had exactly $5,000 to our name at that time.

It was another piece of evidence, noticed and collected, for me to keep trusting my gut. Feeling empowered to follow this unfolding path, and trust the process, I said, "We can sell a car if we need to, or we can drain the savings. We'll figure out the money, let's do it."

By nature a slow mover, the fast pace of this sudden turn of events had proved to be overwhelming for Tim. Knowing how important rebuilding our savings had been to my sense of security after writing the biggest check of our lives for a down payment, Tim wanted to make sure I understood this would wipe us out, dropping us down to $0. He knew I had my heart set on eventually renovating the sad, 1950's galley kitchen, and that would be another dream that had to wait.

He put his head in his hands and said through tears, "I feel like I'm taking everything from you."

I felt another strong sense of knowing, as though I had zoomed out and could, for a moment, hold a much larger perspective. "Tim," I said gently, accessing a deep place within myself, and making sure he was looking at me, "I plan to renovate many kitchens in my life. But I only plan to have one marriage. Let's do it."

We cried together for a moment before Tim said, "Can we just take a second and pray?"

We did, and it was a sweet moment in the midst of great disappointment and pain. This was not the path we'd envisioned when we said, "I do," three years prior. This was not the goal we'd set when we'd bought our first house, or when we'd written and recorded cute, happy, love songs, singing them for strangers in living rooms, churches, and bars across the country; what would they think of us now?

It didn't matter. Something inside both of us knew this was a path worth taking. A path of undoing that would take time and effort before we could even begin the redoing. Our new goal was revealing itself in a question: Do you want to be well?

United in our request for God to care for us, to provide for us as we stood on an invisible ledge, we prayed, asking boldly that the resources we needed, and the healing we desired make their way to us. This moment, pausing together to set an intention, to believe something outside of ourselves was also involved in this free-fall, served to help us release the control we'd been grasping for, and lead us to new levels of surrender, faith, and even hope.

Knowing the clock was ticking on a 5 p.m. deadline, we decided to divide and conquer. If we were going to do this, there were a few arrangements we needed to make and a few people we needed to call. As tempting as it was to hide and isolate in our brokenness, we chose to allow ourselves to be seen and known in a fractured and vulnerable place. In doing so, we experienced a miracle, reminding us of the importance of staying connected. Over the course of the next 30 minutes, as we spoke with several friends that we deeply trusted, somehow, we gathered every penny of the $5,000 for the 5 p.m.

registration deadline, and our savings remained untouched.

The next week was a whirlwind. Dropping Tim off in the middle of nowhere Tennessee, I drove home, alone with my beloved pitbull, Riggins, with the windows down and tears falling freely. Tears of fear, anticipation, relief, hurt, anger, confusion, and hope. As broken as I was, I also felt alive, as though I was on the cusp of something new and undiscovered but terrified of what the path ahead might be. Would we get divorced? Had he cheated on me and just wasn't brave enough to admit it yet? Would the truth I was desperately trying to find, and stand on, shift again under my feet, sending me spinning again, unsure of what was up or down?

I didn't know.
I. Did. Not. Know.

Could I be okay with this? This unknowing, this undoing? Instead of trying to outrun it, fix it, manage it, or turn a blind eye to it in denial, could I trust the process, allowing God to hold me as I experienced it unfold, one slow, small step at a time?

I wanted assurance, absolutes, guarantees. Was he going to get well? What did that mean? How would I know? Was I worth it to him? Did he even want me? Would he relapse? What would I do if he did? Could I stay? But none of those answers were available to me at the moment. It seemed I had to live into them, trusting they would come in time.

Tim was gone for seven days. As Sunday came, I dragged my broken heart to church and sat alone, close to the front in a dark room while the music played. As melodies danced over me, sung by trusted friends, I sensed a question arrive. It felt like God.

Stephanie. Will you let me ruin your marriage?

Isn't it already ruined? I thought, rolling my eyes at the absurdity of the question.

Beloved, I am in the business of trading beauty for ashes. But to arrive at ashes, something first must burn. Are you willing to allow the marriage you've known to fall apart? Stop trying to return to what was, or salvage what's left. I am interested in doing something new. Do you trust me?

In that moment, I felt something inside of me open to both pain and possibility, as I released my grip that I believed was holding my marriage together.

"I trust You," I whispered.

THANK YOU FOR FAILING ME

Chapter 9
Put Your Hand on Your "Knower"

Anthony De Mello writes in his book, The Way to Love[ii], "Here is a mistake that most people make in their relationships with others. They try to build a steady nesting place in the ever-moving stream of life."

De Mello goes on to ask the reader if there is a particular person whose love they desire. "Do you want to be important to this person, to be special and make a difference to his/her life? Do you want this person to care for you and be concerned about you in a special way?"

I'm not sure he could've summed up my desire any better. Yes, to all of it. All the yeses. Sign me up, put me in coach — this was what I had been looking for my whole life! It was like an aroma I carried with me into all my important relationships: Please care for me and be concerned about me in a special way. Of course, for me, the underbelly of that request was: because if you don't, then I guess I'm not worth it.

When Tim and I got married, I had just left the record label of my dreams with my tail between my legs. I felt rejected by the label in a similar way I'd felt rejected by my father. Eventually, they'd just stopped responding, and I grew increasingly convinced it was personal. Naturally, as that relationship was phasing out, I clung to a new one that was forming. When Tim asked me to marry him, I devoured his promise in front of God and community that he would love and care for me, promising never to leave me.

I desperately wanted a steady nesting place. The ever-moving stream of life was too unpredictable, too painful — there had been sharp rocks and violent currents that had pulled me under. I wanted certainty, guarantees, and promises. I especially loved the idea of promises made in front of other people — they made me feel powerful and secure, and I could weaponize them, like a gun pointed to Tim's head saying, "you said you would love and cherish me—YOU SAID! And all these people heard you! Now you HAVE TO!"

Tim and I had never been married before, we did our best to establish a rhythm together, but like any first draft, it needed revisions. The problem was, we had no idea how to renovate what we'd constructed. So, we just dug deeper ruts in the same path, dancing to the same dysfunctional dance that we had co-created.

Our old programming told us that you either got things right, or you got them wrong. We were terrified to get anything "wrong," especially marriage. No one had told us that conflict, struggle, tension, loneliness, hurt, anger, and sadness were actually our teachers. We avoided our own hearts, afraid of what they might reveal to us, and we tried to "play house." Keep dancing, keep dancing, just keep dancing.

With Tim in a weeklong intensive for addiction, our dance had been interrupted. I had always sensed there was more to a life-long commitment than keeping peace and going through the motions, but I hadn't grown up in a home with two parents, modeling how to live whole-heartedly with each other and in the world. I just knew I never wanted to get divorced, so keeping the peace felt like my best option. But there was a small part of me slowly growing to believe this unraveling might be the way forward.

I clung to M. Scott Peck's words, "We must be willing to fail and to appreciate the truth that often, life is not a problem to be solved, but a mystery to be lived." I was finding my willingness to live into the mystery.

***

A few weeks after Tim had returned home from Onsite, the facilitator from his program, Eli Machin, sat across from me in our tiny living room. He had traveled in from Asheville, North Carolina to lead a couple's intensive weekend for a handful of other marriages in triage, much like us. But, as our unfortunate fate at the time would have it, we had a conflict with the dates. When Tim told him we couldn't make it, he surprised us with his response.

Mentioning he rarely did this, he offered to come to our house and provide a private, five-hour session with just us, on the condition we picked him up from the airport and took him to his hotel after, so he didn't have to rent a car. He even offered to give us the "friend rate" and only charge us the equivalent of one month's mortgage payment.

Halfway through the private session in our living room, Eli directed his attention toward me, and I sank deeper into our secondhand Craigslist couch. "Now, this man has some mountains to climb, he's got his work cut out for him," he said pointing to Tim, while not releasing eye contact with me. "I hope he shows up for it—and he'd be a fool not to, he's got a lot to lose if he doesn't, but time will tell." He smiled warmly, winking at me, before adopting a tone I hadn't heard from him yet. "But you've got work to do here too."

I wanted to be perceived as a good student, I wanted to get it right, so I nodded my head in agreement. *Yes, of course—I mean, no one is perfect,* I thought to myself, wondering what exactly he meant. The truth was, other than the "no one is perfect " part, I didn't know what he meant. Sure, I'd lost my temper a few times, but sitting in my own house with a CSAT (Certified Sex Addiction Therapist) across from me, I felt like this had all been done to me. I hadn't been looking at porn on my phone while Tim slept innocently next to me. I hadn't been the one that incited a trip to the community health center for STD testing. What work did I have to do?

Eli could see I didn't understand. "I'd like to lead you in an exercise," he said leaning forward in his chair as though it was about to get good.

"We are all physical, emotional, and spiritual beings. When something is true, we know it in our minds, but we also know it in our bodies." He waited for me to agree before asking, "When you know something is true, where in your body do you feel it? Some people get a tingle down their arms, others, their feet ache. Mine is in my lower belly. Everyone has a place in their body they can feel when something is true. For our purposes here, we'll call that your 'knower.' Stephanie, where is your 'knower?'"

It sounded a little woo-woo, but I couldn't argue with him. The last few weeks my 'knower' had been on fire, prompting me to ask questions when I sensed I didn't have the whole story, inviting me to practice trust on this new path unfolding slowly before me; and each time, my 'knower' had been right.

I sat quietly, noticing that when I encountered something true, I felt a warm expansion in my chest. My 'knower' was at my center, just under my clavicle and just above my sternum. "Here," I whispered as I placed my hand there.

"Good!" Eli said. "Keep your hand there, and next I want you to ask your Higher Power what He thinks about you. Take your time but speak it out when you know something."

Grateful my eyes were closed so I could roll them privately, my first reaction was that this exercise was beneath me. *This is dumb. I was raised in church — I already know God loves me, blah blah* — but my cynicism was interrupted as a second thought arrived.

Stephanie! You are paying this guy a buttload of money right now, could you maybe just TRY and participate? Deep breath. Okay. I'll try.

After an extensive pause, I responded to his question like a question. "Lovely?" Still nervous to get it wrong, I spoke the only word that had bubbled to the surface after I began to feel self-conscious about how long I'd been silent, warring with myself to engage in the exercise.

"Yes! What else?" Eli asked, inviting me to dig around in my 'knower' a little more.

I deflated slightly, realizing the exercise wasn't done. I closed my eyes again, hand still on my chest, a little annoyed that my first answer wasn't sufficient. *God, what else do you say about me? Please don't be silent.* On some level, I was afraid I might not hear anything, and I didn't know if I could handle God ignoring me too.

I noticed my hand still resting on my chest. Feeling my lungs expand, I tried to drop from my brain that was hovering above the experience — observing it and worrying about "right" and "wrong" — down into my being, my 'knower,' that was the experience. I tried to remember a time I'd sensed something was true about me. "Daughter," I said with more confidence this time.

"Ah, yes. That's beautiful. You belong. Great, what else?"

Okay, I'm catching on here. My obsession about getting this right was subduing and curiosity grew as I wondered what else might come up.

"I'm wanted," I said, sensing more of a feeling than a word this time.

"Good! You matter, you are desired. That's great," Eli said, his own excitement growing as he asked one more question, "I want you to ask God if God likes you."

This time, I saw an image in my mind, followed by a statement. A face, exploding with joy and an open-mouthed smile. A laugh erupting from a head tilted back in delight. *Stephanie, you are such a good hang.*

"I think God just said I was a good hang?" I offered, wondering where we would go from here.

"And do you often say that about people you don't like?" Eli smiled and gave the room space before making his final point. "So, the God of the Universe just said you were loved, you belonged, you mattered, and that you were a good hang. Can anything this man does—or doesn't do—change that?" He motioned to Tim as he raised an eyebrow for emphasis. Elaborating on his opening statement to me, he saw that I was getting it now. "Stephanie, your work is believing what is already true. This man, nor any other man, can't touch what God has already established unless you stop believing it. So yes, you have work here. Stop accepting unacceptable behavior from others. Your work is believing, and believing is hard work."

My brain was on fire. It was as if I saw colors I'd never seen before. My awareness grew like a flower opening in a time-lapse video. New insights and perspectives, previously hidden in plain sight, were all around me. For the first time, I could see my participation in the dysfunctional pattern that seemed to be on repeat in my life.

I had made a habit of giving away my birthright—my worthiness—and asking someone else to care for it. That is far too heavy a load for another to hold. When they inevitably wavered on caring for me perfectly, I assigned meaning to their actions: I wasn't worth it. I had made caring for my soul, and appraising my value, someone else's responsibility. But my value was never up for a vote, yet I had been polling all of creation—my family of origin, my art and abilities, my relationships—desperate for some outcome that would silence the fear that I was inherently unwanted.

I had forgotten what had always been true: I was loved, I belonged, and I mattered. Something bigger than me had always wanted me here—even enjoyed my company it seemed. My sheer existence was proof of that. Perhaps I was a surprise to my fellow creation (my parents), but I had not been a surprise to God. I'd always been wanted. A Higher Power had placed me into the ongoing creation story in 1984 and had been inviting me to participate in its unfolding ever since.

I suddenly realized no one could believe enough for me. Yes, we should affirm the good, beauty, and significance we see in others, but the praise of others will always leave us thirsty again. There was an inexhaustible Source of Love available to me that I could connect with and never deplete with my neediness. The same Source that had instigated my existence and sustained me all this time, who was the Giver of every good thing.

This was my work to practice—to return to and remain in the love that had always been mine.

As it applied to my current situation, I began to see options available to me that I had never noticed—or perhaps had never been willing to consider.

If I was worth caring for, why had I accepted unacceptable behavior for so long? In my fear of being a divorcee, like my mother, and my vow to make it work at any cost, I had sequentially lost myself in my marriage. I had blown my individual candle out. That was suddenly too expensive of a cost. I'd placed the care of my soul in the hands of everyone around me for too long. Was I willing to accept the responsibility to care well for myself? And what the hell did that look like?

For the first time, it occurred to me that if Tim didn't want to get well, that was about him, not me. It didn't mean I wasn't worth it, it just meant he didn't want to do the work to get well. He was free to choose how he wanted to proceed, and he would either choose to get well or he wouldn't. For the first time, instead of fearing that discovery, it suddenly felt like that would be valuable information to acquire, and the only way to gather it would be to get out of the way and watch what happened. But for it to come to me honestly, I had to stop trying to manipulate the outcome. I had to give Tim the chance to fail… or succeed.

That meant allowing him to be himself, to think his thoughts, feel his feelings, and behave in any way that he decided to (because in reality, people will think, feel, and do what they want. They'll just hide it from us if they think we can't handle it). Thinking that I had any control over someone else was an illusion.

While this concept terrified me, I could see how my grip had tightened around my marriage. Of course, I hadn't been able to release Tim when I was using him to assess my value. I'd just wanted him to modify his behavior, so I could bear staying married to him and wouldn't have to face taking healthy action for myself. But none of it was working. I thought back to God's question to me, "Stephanie, are you willing to let me ruin your marriage?" Perhaps this is what that looked like?

To be clear, I still loved Tim, and I wanted to be married to him. But I was no longer going to beg him to love me or to get well. What if I didn't actually need to die slowly in an unhealthy marriage, bound by fear that I wouldn't be loved, belong, or matter—let alone that God wouldn't like me—if my marriage ended?

Something was changing in me rapidly; I was filled with a peace I couldn't explain. It wasn't that I knew my marriage would be okay. It was that, for the first time, I knew I would be okay, no matter what.

I was in a free fall, but instead of worrying about where or how I was going to land, I was growing in confidence that regardless of where I landed, it would be good.

De Mello finishes with this: "(When you release another), you set yourself free. You are now ready to love. For when you cling, what you offer the other is not love but a chain by which both you and your beloved are bound. Love can only exist in freedom. The true lover seeks the good of his beloved which requires especially the liberation of the beloved from the lover."[iii]

I was unchaining myself from Tim, giving him space to choose to love me—or not. I had to release him because love is free. I cannot make someone love me. I cannot control what another thinks or feels. As my awareness grew that I was already loved, I noticed I was able to differentiate between 'Tim deciding he didn't love me' and 'not being lovable.' I'd been asking the wrong question. If the question wasn't whether I was lovable, but rather 'does the person I'm with treat me in a loving way?' then I wasn't as afraid of the answer. Although it wasn't the world I wanted, I was beginning to imagine a world where I would be okay, even if Tim didn't want me anymore.

***

Eli coined many kitschy terms that became fluent in our vernacular, one of which was "knower" and another which was: "the show up place." By Eli's definition, to "show up in the show up place" meant to metaphorically come out of the weeds, buck-ass naked. To stand exposed, vulnerable, unhidden, and unguarded. The risky thing about showing up is you don't know if the other person will meet you there. You certainly hope they do—you even invite them to—but they may not. You may be left lonely and exposed.

Conversely, however, you also may experience the wonder of true connection, because the other might just show up as well. And the beauty, intimacy, and trust that occurs when another does step out of hiding and joins you—buck-ass naked, guard down, willing to be seen and known—is nothing short of precious.

Eli told us if only one person shows up over a matter of time, being left lonely and exposed over and over, it is too unbearable, and they will eventually stop showing up. I related to that. I had begun our marriage showing up, but over and over, I was left lonely. Eventually, I couldn't bear it anymore. I wasn't sure Tim even knew how to find the show up place, so I had grown protected and guarded myself. With our marriage on the line however, he had recently proved me wrong. First by writing me spontaneous and heartfelt love notes nearly every day, and second, by agreeing to a formal disclosure.

A formal disclosure involves professionals who help guide couples through the painful revealing of information that has previously been withheld. Tim combed through his story with the help of his therapist, answering my questions and filling in holes in the story regarding his sexual past. It is meant to be a "fresh start" of sorts, the idea being that once everything is on the table—no more secrets, no more hiding—couples can begin building a new foundation on a level, clean slate.

We had a messy first round of disclosure, and although it was unprecedented, our therapists both agreed to do a second. If I was learning anything on this path, it was that sometimes it takes a few attempts to get where you're going. You may find yourself face down in the mud, but when you're ready, you can dust yourself off and try again.

One of the ways we began rebuilding trust, and learning how to show up with each other, was intentionally checking in using an acronym called FANOS.

Feelings
Affirmation
Needs
Ownership
Sobriety

Every day on Tim's lunch break, he would call, and we would take a few minutes to come out of hiding and be known to each other. We'd offer any of the eight core feelings (anger, hurt, sad, lonely, fear, guilt, shame, glad) that had dominated our day. Explanations were optional and clarifying questions could be asked, but it was good practice, first in reawakening to the hearts we'd fallen asleep to, and second, in vulnerably offering what we found to another. It not only built trust, but it also built intimacy, as we learned not to fear our own emotions or each other's.

Next, we'd offer one small affirmation of the other, big or small. It could be something as simple as "I noticed you put an extra dollar in the tip jar at the coffee shop, you are generous." The 'Needs' category could be a request, like "I need your help with ___" or a statement along the lines of, "I need to exercise today."

Ownership is to pull the curtain back, turn the lights on, and expose ourselves for the imperfect beings that we are. Tim, who had begun a 12-step recovery program, got a sponsor that would start a call with: "What have you done, and what are you thinking about doing?" Obviously, discretion must be used here when speaking with your spouse. I didn't need to know every dirty thought that popped in my husband's head, but it did help to re-establish trust when he offered something like, "I'm struggling today, I'm feeling really triggered. But I want you to know I've bookended my day with calls to my sponsor and he's aware that it's a hard day." Sometimes ownership looked like, "I flipped off the driver who cut me off today and am still nursing that resentment, but that's a dangerous place for me, so I've got to own it."

Finally, the "S" stands for sobriety. This gives the addict an opportunity to take responsibility for their own recovery and give a daily update of their sobriety. If there is a slip or a relapse, they have twenty-four hours to own it before it's considered hiding. This provides an opportunity for the spouse of the addict to practice their work of not managing, over-asking, or snooping—after all, they are NOT responsible for the addict's sobriety. But it also builds trust in the result of a slip, though it might be painful to hear, it reveals that the addict can, in fact, tell the truth about hard things. Although a mistake was made, it shows they are still committed to a lifestyle of recovery and not hiding.

One time Tim called on a Wednesday morning after an early meeting before work. We chatted as he drove 20 minutes to the office of his new job before saying goodbye and wishing each other a nice day. I was surprised to see his name pop up on my phone just seconds after hanging up the first call.

"Hello?" I answered curiously.

"I have an ownership to make. I lied to you. I told you I stopped for a coffee and a donut, but..." he paused, as if he was struggling to spit it out.

Shit. Did he get the barista's number? My traumatized brain immediately went to the worst-case scenario.

"I got two donuts," he confessed with an exhale.

I laughed, probably more than was appropriate as I disguised my relief as nonchalance. "Timmy, that's okay! You don't have to own that—"

"Well, I do. Here's why," Tim nearly cut me off, needing me to understand. "I feel some shame about eating two. I've gained a little weight recently, and I'm not happy about my body. The story I told you was calculated, I altered reality to make myself sound better, like I had more self-control than I actually did. When you didn't question it, I felt like I got away with something, and it felt good. That's not a healthy place for me, so I just wanted to own it and tell you the truth."

This moment was the first glimpse I had at this man becoming my teacher. One day at a time, I noticed he was committed to a new way of showing up in his own life. Though I'd doubted he was even capable of it, here he was offering the truth without me having to dig for it. Living from a place of rigorous honesty meant he exposed his sideways motives to the light before they had a chance to grow. Jordan Peterson says, "Slay the dragon when its flames are that of a Bic lighter." Tim knew what it was like to nurse a secret, compounding them as they grew larger and larger. In active repentance, he was learning not to expect perfection from himself, rather, to realign with truth once he became aware that he'd mis-stepped.

Telling the truth about seemingly small things helped us begin to re-establish a foundation of trust to stand on. Our world had suddenly become small and simple, we were not on a stage or in a different city every night, performing for approval. Instead, we were cooking meals together and having dinner at a real table, instead of in front of a TV, getting to know each other, in many ways, for the first time.

Chapter 10
Joining A Club No One Wants To Be Part Of

During this season of undoing, Tim and I experienced a wide pendulum of highs and lows. The whole thing was fragile and unpredictable. A romantic meal could easily be hijacked by heightened emotions and words intended to wound.

I was baffled by the perpetual car accident we were. Even with best intentions, I kept getting blindsided, resulting in mangled and shattered expectations. Surely, one of these blows would be the end of me eventually.

When the brain is healing from trauma that's been stored in the body for years, it's bound to be messy. As old and faulty narratives unravel, untethering you from the way you once understood the world and your place in it, it's easy to feel vulnerable and exposed, unsure of who is for you or against you. Even your spouse can feel like an adversary.

Tim was establishing his new normal, consisting of 90 recovery meetings in 90 days and weekly counseling with a specialized therapist. He was getting support from fellow travelers on a similar path, encouraging him that by detaching from coping mechanisms that no longer served him well, he might come to experience a new and freer way of being. But this new way was coming slowly, and the path seemed much more like a mountainous zigzag than a linear straight shot.

With the chaos of the initial disclosure and discovery settling, the rug wasn't being pulled out from under me every few days with new secrets coming to light, but I was still struggling to find my footing. I tend to kick ass in a crisis, but when the dust begins to settle and the adrenaline fades, it never fails to surprise me that I am still but a human and often need help processing what I've been through.

Over coffee one morning in her kitchen, my friend Leslie delivered some truth to me in a way only a trusted friend can. "Steph, I think you've walked through hell in the past few weeks. I am so glad Tim is finding his way and doing well, but I sense some PTSD in your language, and it might be good to give your soul some care too. Have you thought about seeing a counselor yourself?"

I felt exposed, perhaps embarrassed, that I hadn't demonstrated more superhuman strength, as I desperately wanted to be considered "doing well" by onlookers, and secretly hoped I could earn a gold star for walking through hard things on my own.

Thankfully, there were many sweet years of friendship equity banked with Leslie, and because I trusted her, I could surrender my ego and hear her. I knew she was for me, and I knew she was right. But I didn't know where to begin looking for a therapist, plus our finances were going towards Tim's individual therapy, and we were barely covering our bills.

I told her I'd consider it in a few weeks when we figured out jobs, since it was clear we wouldn't be touring anytime soon.

Later that evening, I received a text that read: "Steph, I spoke with Thomas, and we want to give you $1000 for your own healing. That should get you about ten sessions with someone. I hope it helps; you are worth it friend. Love you."

As my head collapsed in my hands, I mentally "file-saved" another example of God's provision. I had lived so much of my life in scarcity. Without even realizing it, my default was often an impaired belief that there wasn't enough for me. Enough money, love, opportunity, or resources. Little by little, I was waking up to the beautiful reality that I didn't have to know where my help was coming from, only remain open to receiving it.

There is an ancient Hebrew story where Jesus asked the man at the pool of Bethesda a question that kept ringing around in my head: "Do you want to be well?" The man responds by saying, "No one will help me!" But that's not what Jesus asked, he didn't ask, "Why haven't you gotten well yet?" Perhaps Jesus knew the man was looking for someone else to do the work for him, so he instructed him to pick up his mat and walk, almost as if to say, "Are you willing to participate in your own healing?"

With nothing but time on my hands, and now the financial means to see someone, I knew the invitation to get well was in front of me. It was time to pick up my mat and walk.

That's how I found Laura. Laura was spunky, had amazing hair, and broke just enough rules that I respected her but kept just enough that I trusted her. If we were allowed to be friends outside of her office, I'd like to think that we would have been. But alas, that was one rule she kept—no outside friendships with clients.

Laura was an advocate for women in crisis. Many of her clients were married to addicts, some of them addicts themselves. She helped me identify that I towed the line of love-addict and codependent myself, and one of the first things she told me was, "Of my clients that get well, the ones that go to 12 step meetings get there faster."

I had already begun to see a shift in Tim since he'd been going to meetings. And I didn't love the idea of being part of a club that no one ever dreamt about joining, but I remembered Eli's words to me, "You have work to do too." If there was fullness of life, or freedom to be found in those rooms, I wanted it. Like Jamie George said at my wedding, it's part of my nature to gulp life, not sip it. I was willing to try anything, so I began going to 12 step meetings myself.

I learned quickly that I qualified for a program long before I met Tim. I'd spent my whole life trying not to marry my father, but as it turns out, I'd married my mother's father, my grandfather, Ken, the man who helped raise me. I didn't know it growing up, but he'd been a man with secrets himself. Secrets that had surfaced shortly before his passing in 2005 and had challenged my understanding of love. I'd come to terms that his love for me, and his family, wasn't canceled or less valuable because of his reckless behavior. He was a complicated man, capable of both loving and hurting the ones he loved very deeply. No wonder I hadn't thought to be more concerned about Tim's hidden persona, it's what had been modeled for me. It turns out, I came by my character defects of denial, control, obsessing, manipulating, and accepting unacceptable behavior, quite honestly.

In recovery rooms, I learned that I shared the "problem" with other members, as the literature for my fellowship reads:

"Most of us grew up in families with secrets, and we were not taught to think about our own needs and take positive action to meet them. We chose friends and partners who could not or would not love and support us in a healthy way. We lived life from the standpoint of victims and perceived any personal criticism as a threat. For most of us, anger, fear, and depression were nearly constant. We acquired some unhealthy beliefs about ourselves very early in our lives – that we were not worthwhile and lovable, that we were able to control other people's behavior, and that sex was the most important sign of love."[iv]

OKAY! WHO READ MY JOURNAL? It was like fireworks were going off in my consciousness. No one had made me marry this guy, I had done it of my own free will. I was the one who chose a partner who didn't know how to love and support me in a healthy way. That didn't mean Tim's actions were a result of anything I had or hadn't done. It didn't mean I was stupid, weak, or unattractive; it just meant I didn't have the power to control any of his behavior, but to some degree I'd thought I did. Over time, as I tried to control or ignore his addiction, I'd unknowingly acted in ways that led to a further decline in my own emotional health.

The program literature kept referring to the addict as a "sick person, not a bad person." It helped me offer grace to Tim, my grandfather, even my own father; they weren't bad, they were sick. The more I kept the focus on myself, I began to see the ways that I, too, had become spiritually and emotionally ill. And I began to see that I did have choices. This was the beginning of my recovery.

For example, my brain knew I deserved more than what Tim was giving me in my marriage, and my mouth even came to the party and had no trouble telling him to do better. The problem was my actions revealed that I didn't believe it, at least not to the depths where I would take healthy action for myself. That's why when—over and over—he didn't follow through or care better for me, I accepted it. Why had I accepted unacceptable behavior for so long? Clearly there was a disconnect between my head knowledge and what I believed. If I actually believed I deserved to be cared for better, I wouldn't have settled for the table scraps I'd been scavenging for.

As I continued to see Laura, I noticed she had a way of simplifying chaos for me. When I would get stuck in my familiar "What am I going to do — Is my marriage going to make it?" loop, she'd respond with, "One day at a time. Tim needs at least three months to get sober, and then another three to make any real progress. So, keep doing your work — get clear on what is, and isn't, acceptable to you and hold your ground. Don't make any big decisions for at least six months, and just know: sober looks different. You haven't even met him sober yet. Give him a chance to sober up, and you will know what you need to know, when you need to know it."

That made sense to me. I wasn't in danger, I was uncomfortable. There were days I wanted to throw in the towel, but I also wanted to see if he would do his work — if he wanted this as much as I did. I was realizing I couldn't want it enough for him, he had to choose to get well — and he was either going to, or he wasn't. That was good information to have. But it would take time to know, and as they say in the rooms: Time takes time.

On my worst days, when I felt particularly lonely or afraid of my future, I would ask myself, *Can you make it to lunch today?* Somehow, I'd make it to lunch. Then I'd set a new goal; *Can you make it to bed? Let's just finish this day and worry about tomorrow, tomorrow.*

Sure enough, without fail, time did pass. And in each moment, I found I had what I needed. Moments came and went, until a bunch of moments became a day. Then day by day, week by week, and month by month, a new way of being emerged. I started gathering data, noticing I was able to find serenity even when my life was painful or hard. Instead of living in denial or avoidance, I was facing some of my biggest fears, and they weren't killing me. I started to see how, "This too shall pass" meant good moments, as well as hard. That nothing lasts forever. I could hold loosely to sweet moments, trusting that when they passed, more goodness would come eventually. And I could endure pain, heartache, disappointment, and fear more than I'd ever realized, standing in confidence that it wouldn't last forever.

I've heard it said, "The whole Universe is rigged in favor of your growth." I think it's true that everything is, in fact, my teacher, if I'm willing to be taught. Sometimes I just need a little help finding the lesson.

Chapter 11
Who Knew I Really Sucked at Boundaries?

Another way Laura assisted me in growing up, was to better understand boundaries. That was a doozie for me. I was great at setting boundaries; I could run my mouth and say, "You can't treat me like that!" But I had no idea that holding my boundaries was also my responsibility. *Who knew?!* I thought it was everyone else's job—because surely, they would respect my boundaries if they loved me, right? I also had never been taught that boundaries also meant you respected other people's, even if you thought their boundaries were dumb. To this day, I can hear Laura in my head saying, "Boundaries are three-fold—setting, holding, and respecting. If you're not good at all of the three, you're not good at boundaries."

Peter Crone says, "Life will present you with people and circumstances to reveal where you are not free."ᵛ *Ugh, don't you hate him a little for that? Me too. But he's right.*

When Tim was touring with House of Heroes, they traveled the country in a van and trailer. But when they slowed down, each got married, and took other jobs, guess who became the storage yard for the ugly, well-traveled, eyesore of metal and rubber? This girl. For five years, it sat dormant and taking up space in my driveway. "Can someone else in the band park it at their house? Can you sell it? It's an eyesore, no one uses it, and your band is wasting money paying insurance on it!" I pleaded, reasoned, rationed. Tim would agree, they needed to sell it, and I would settle down for a while, hoping he'd act this time, and follow through (because he loved me, right?). Yet there it was.

I felt my hands were tied; this wasn't my van. I wasn't on the title or in the band. I had inherited it with my marriage, and Tim had it long before me. I felt powerless over taking any action myself, and I felt unheard and unimportant when Tim seemed to ignore my requests. But once I was a year or two into recovery and therapy, I decided to practice some of the boundary work I was learning. At the time, we were renovating a storage room into a studio apartment to Airbnb in our basement—*yes, it does have glitter floors*—and the impending deadline felt like I could try again with the van, so I said to Tim, "We have one month until our first guest arrives. That van needs to be gone by then so they can park in the driveway." Tim agreed and I added, "If it's not gone, I will be until it is."

"Okay, it'll get done." Tim confirmed.

There was a deadline, and it had been agreed upon. Plus, there was an expectation set for what would happen if he didn't follow through. From there, I tried to let it go and not "mommy wife" or manage it for him. Channeling my inner Brené Brown, I borrowed one of her mantras: "Don't puff up, don't shrink, just stand your sacred ground."

As the agreed upon date approached, I was beginning to sweat. I had been clear on the front end that I was more than willing to help, but I would not be running point on the operation. There had been no further discussion. And as the weeks passed… crickets.

I went to a recovery meeting and shared about the fast-arriving deadline for the van's exodus. After the meeting, a wise friend who'd been in the program longer than me asked why would I be the one leaving my own home? "Because I can't make Tim leave," I responded, confident there were only two options, and I had selected the correct one; either he leaves, or I leave.

"Is that the only thing you have control over?" she asked, leaving it there.

In one simple question, she shorthand-serenity-prayer-ed the crap out of me! "God, grant me the serenity to accept the things I cannot change, courage to change the things I can, and wisdom to know the difference."

Like a lightbulb illuminating above my head, I saw it! Something *else* could leave. This felt familiar. I'd been here before. Eli had asked why I took the air mattress when we separated in our home. In both scenarios, I had wanted my potential absence to be what scared Tim into action. I was still making this about my value to him! I was trying to control, using myself as the pawn.

This didn't have to be personal. What if it was as simple as: we are different people and therefore different things are important to us. Why did I need him to validate what was important to me? Perhaps he just didn't mind the van taking up space and I did. Could that be okay? And could that be enough of a reason for me to act on moving it? It wasn't my van, but it was my driveway. I was allowed to want it gone, and there was something I could do to make it leave my property.

When I got home, I asked Tim if it was a good time to talk. I told him I needed to make an adjustment to the boundary I'd made regarding the van and trailer. Internally reciting one of my favorite slogans: *Say what you mean. Mean what you say. But don't say it mean*, I was calm as I opened the topic. "As you know, our first guest arrives in less than a week now." Tim nodded, seeming unfazed. "Originally I'd said that I would be leaving to stay with a friend if the van wasn't moved, but I'm making an amendment to that." Tim seemed more interested in what I had to say now. "I wanted to let you know that if the van is still here on Friday, I will have it towed, and your band will pay to have it moved somewhere else, because it won't be coming back here."

Tim's eyes darkened, and I swear smoke came out of his ears. I made the choice to stay calm, even to be kind. We were learning a new dance here. I had been a pushover for a long time, and I knew this was stepping on his toes. But I didn't want to keep suffocating what I wanted. I reminded him that I'd been asking for years, I'd been patient, and there was still plenty of time to have a different outcome here. There were still five days to take some action, and I was willing to help however he needed.

I wish I could say that went over well. Buuuuuuuut, it was messy. Tim threw a grown-man temper-tantrum before leaving for Home Depot for two hours. When he did eventually come home, he walked briskly past me as I worked at the dining room table. Not even glancing in my direction, he spoke to the air in front of him, "I'm not ready to talk yet."

I wanted to shrink, erupt, or apologize — anything to relieve the tension. But more so, I wanted to try something new. I chose my tone carefully and said, "Let me know when you are," as I practiced 'detaching in love' as the program says. Just because he was having a moment, didn't mean I had to join the chaos. I could stay present with myself, and trust that he would show up when he was ready. I was learning to ask for what was wanted or needed without being mean, passive aggressive, or mousey. But sometimes I did have to be patient. After another 30 minutes, he came and sat across from me at the table.

I often think back to Laura's words, "Sober looks different." She was right; I knew when I was talking with sober-minded, adult Tim and when I was not. Sometimes, it's evident that a younger version of Tim is possessing his limbic system, but I could tell he was fully present with me as his recovered-self now. We were both calm as we addressed the hot topic between us. Tim began, assuring me he heard me and knew the van and trailer needed to go, and he took ownership that he had failed to follow through on it many times. He helped me understand that the van was quite complicated for him. The title was missing somewhere in Ohio, and he felt lonely shouldering the burden alone for the band. He also offered that there was a part of him that had been avoiding the task all together because so much of his identity had been wrapped up in touring, but that season was ending. In some ways he didn't have to face it entirely if they had the option to tour. The van and trailer, along with all the gear and merch still in the trailer, was the anchor keeping them tethered to a former life as rockstars.

This made sense to me, and I had wondered if there was more to it than inconvenience. I reminded him again that I was his biggest fan and wanted to help him, he didn't have to do it alone, but I did want to find a new arrangement for at least that trailer. That sparked an idea for me! If we could find another place for the trailer, the van would fit in our carport, clearing the driveway for our guests. It felt like a healthy compromise to break the inertia.

Together, we devised a plan. Another band member would store the trailer while Tim found the title to the van. He would also begin the discussion with the band about dividing the gear and merch from the trailer so we could sell it. Forward motion always feels so good after you've been stuck for a while.

A week later, my neighbor and good friend Jayme stopped by. She noticed the van was moved and the trailer was gone. I told her we were in the process of downsizing our real estate in motor vehicles, and she immediately asked if her boss could buy the van. He was looking to buy something for his hotdog business and was willing to do a handshake deal until the new title came from Ohio. He picked it up the next day and suddenly, there was no van or trailer on my property!

When we begin this work, it can be a little clumsy. Adapting and amending our boundaries as we learn is okay, and it may be a little messy at times. Sometimes your dance partner doesn't know the moves to your new dance, and you're bound to step on each other's toes! That's okay. Stay open, don't shut down. Your perspective might not be wrong, only limited. Ask for help and be willing to learn. When my current reality wasn't working for me, I began to dare to ask the question: What else is possible?

Instead of finding the answer by modifying someone else's behavior, I found it in changing my own. But I first had to become aware of what I was doing. I can't say it better than **Twelve Steps and Twelve Traditions**, so I'll quote this short reading.

> "Either we insist upon dominating the people we know, or we depend upon them far too much. If we lean too heavily on people, they will sooner or later fail us, for they are human, too, and cannot possibly meet our incessant demands. In this way, our insecurity grows and festers. When we habitually try to manipulate others to our own willful desires, they revolt, and resist us heavily. Then we develop hurt feelings, a sense of persecution, and a desire to retaliate. As we redouble in our efforts at control, and continue to fail, our suffering becomes acute and constant." [vi]

As I was putting some pieces together in my marriage, noticing how emotionally insecure I had been and the impact that had on the relationship, I began expanding the frame. If Tim sincerely loved me, but still let me down sometimes, perhaps that was true about others. What if I was loved the whole time, and people sometimes failed me because they were people? What if no one could live up to my "incessant demands" of them never hurting me? My dad, my childhood idol, and my husband: all merely fallible humans. No single person can be the supplier of all my hopes, expectations, needs, and wants.

What if a new boundary I needed to set, hold, and respect was… with myself? For years, my bad habit was to lose myself in another, and I was learning that as painful as it could be at times, perhaps the greatest gift another could give me was to fail to shoulder the burden of my sense of self, resulting in my own awakening to it. I was learning to no longer expect other people to provide me with an identity or a sense of self-worth. I was finding the courage to not fail myself.

Chapter 12
Coconut Coffee

It was a lazy Sunday morning. Tim and I begrudgingly emerged from the cocoon of our warm bed to face a cool morning, trying to make it to church with all the other 9 a.m. Jesus-followers.

Running behind, after opting for several alarm snoozes, Tim announced he desperately needed a shower before we left and wouldn't be able to offer me the Chemex pour-over I'd become accustomed to receiving.

But... my coffee? I thought to myself, feeling slighted.

Instead of protesting, I decided to face my fears of the complex brewing process. "Want me to make coffee?" I asked, as he stepped into the shower.

"Aww babe," he paused to look me in the eye, one naked foot already in the steaming shower. "That's really sweet of you, thank you! I'd love to have your coffee." He said it with such sincerity, I almost melted.

Feeling domestic and appreciated, I threw on some clothes, touched up the mascara I had slept in, and made my way to the kitchen.

Yes, there's a food scale and timer involved in this process, and no, I couldn't be bothered to look up the exact measurements. Look, I was sure it would taste like coffee, ok, so I began my brewing process.

Somewhere in between putting the grinder away and the first pour, I second guessed my measurements and decided to use a handy feature, called a "Google search," only to discover I was 4g short on coffee grinds. *Would 4g matter?* I wasn't sure, but I didn't want weak coffee. I also didn't want to get the grinder back out for only 4g, so I grabbed some pre-ground coconut flavored coffee that I had on hand, just for me, in the afternoons.

It seems important to mention here that Tim hates coconut anything.

He'll never taste 4g worth of coconut, I reasoned to myself, *it'll be fine!*

The coffee was waiting when Tim emerged from the bathroom, dressed and ready to go with towel dried hair. As we hurried out the door, he told me again how much he appreciated me making coffee.

He was so dang tender, I felt close to him at that moment. Not to mention, how seen and appreciated I felt. I'd make coffee everyday if I got this kind of affirmation!

From behind the wheel, Tim continued telling me about the podcast he'd been listening to in the shower when abruptly, he stopped talking and sniffed the air.

Sniff. Sniff. "Do you smell coconut?" he asked curiously.

"No! That's weird!" I responded, before I realized words were even on my slippery tongue.

The little lie jumped out so quickly, it was as if I'd spit out a frog. I surprised myself; I didn't even know it was in me. But alas, there it was, my little amphibian of a fib, sitting on the dashboard, staring back at me as we drove, silently questioning my character.

You'd think, given Tim's incredible example of truth-telling of late, it would have been easy for me to confess my indiscretion. But no. I panicked. The lie was out. Deflect, avoid, and cover up seemed my only options.

"What were you saying about a podcast?" I gaslit Tim, hoping his spidey-smelling-senses would settle down. He hadn't even taken a sip yet, how in the world did he smell coconut? It was such a small amount. There was just no way he could know.

Completely unsuspecting of my deception, he dove right back into his podcast story, and I sunk a little deeper into my seat, trying to silence the pit forming in my stomach.

Finding a break in his monologue, Tim reached for his coffee and pressed it to his lips. Before drinking, he sniffed the steam pouring out through the lid.

"You don't smell coconut?" he asked, this time slightly unsure of himself; should he trust his senses or his wife?

"Ohhh, you know what." I said, thinking fast to fabricate a story on the fly that would support him drinking this freaking cup of coffee — as I had unconsciously attached all of his affection to the consumption of it. "I think the creamer I'm using right now has coconut in it. You're probably getting some strong whiffs of mine in the car."

I looked right at him, hoping he would buy my explanation as I watched his eyes dart from the road, to me, to the coffee in his hand, still unsipped. He hesitated, looking conflicted.

Why hadn't I just said, "Ohhhh, you know what? I did use the tiniest bit of coconut coffee this morning. I'm so sorry." Any version of the truth would have been better than looking him in the eye and lying to his face.

Don't bother me now, I demanded to the growing nagging in my conscious. *Yes, I know I just offered a second lie to support my first lie... No, I do not plan on fessing up. Listen, this is just our life now. He must drink this coffee!*

I felt sick to my stomach as I watched him make some inward resolve to trust me. He shrugged his shoulders, abandoned his own senses, and took his first sip.

Wrinkling his nose and nearly spewing the tiny bit he'd consumed, he pushed the beverage in question toward me, eliciting my help, "Taste this! There's definitely coconut in it!"

Still hoping this would go away if I continued my denial, I stayed the course. I took the Yeti, sipped from the nearly untouched edge, and offered the most semi-true statement I could muster, "Hmm, I can't really taste objectively, mine tastes so different with the cream in it."

Handing the tumbler back to Tim, I couldn't look at him. I couldn't bear the thought of him being disappointed in me. After being ignored for some time, my conscious resurfaced, surprising me with a new approach.

Stephanie, this man recently exposed every skeleton in his closet to you, offering you the whole truth of his being, and you can't tell the truth about 4g of coffee?

Like a gut punch, that got my attention.

Tim and I were still recovering from the bruises of broken trust. It had only been a year since the secrets surfaced. With Tim serving as gatekeeper of said secrets, those unexpected truth-bomb-visitors were not surprises to him, only me. To keep them secret, he had lied. Then to maintain the first lie, he'd lied some more, until eventually, he tried something new; he told the truth.

Ironically, in this moment, sitting conflicted in the passenger seat, Tim's willingness to be known in his brokenness was my teacher and my invitation. I was inspired by the courage it must've taken him. Instead of hiding behind another lie, he had bravely offered me the truth. He'd risked losing me in exchange for the gift of reality. Yes, the truth had been painful, but I still wanted it. And him. I really did love him. He'd deemed me safe enough to expose his humanity to. I wondered if maybe he was a safe place too?

We were five minutes from our destination, and this moment of courage needed to be acted upon, lest I talk myself out of it. I knew that I alone was responsible for my character, and to expect the truth from others, I needed to be a truth teller myself.

Ugh—because I'm dramatic, I contorted my body into a ball in the passenger seat as we exited the interstate, and announced, "I'm in my own personal hell over here!"

Correctly interpreting my theatrics as sincere, Tim came to a stop at the red light, turned to face me, and asked if I was okay.

"I have to tell you something!" I confessed, still in pretzel form.

His eyes lit up as if he'd cracked a code, "There WAS coconut in the coffee?!" he exclaimed.

"Yes!" I explained, "I was 4g short, and I didn't think you'd taste it. I'm soooorrry!"

"I KNEW IT!" Tim was laughing, seemingly relieved to know he wasn't crazy.

Relaxing as the tension I'd been feeling released, I knew the confession was only part of my amends. I needed to take responsibility for my dishonesty too.

"I'm sorry I lied to you Timmy," I offered with a more serious tone. "The first one came out so fast, it was done before I even knew I did it. Then I felt like I had to hide behind it, so I kept lying." I looked at him and paused before continuing. "You know, I feel like I under-stand you more after that experience. I can't believe how hard it was to tell you the truth about COFFEE. And you told me the truth about your whole story. I know that wasn't easy for you, but I'm so grateful you did."

A gentle soul, Tim put his warm hand on my leg as he breathed in deeply and took his time before speaking. "Oh babe, that means so much to me. Thank you for that. And yes, unfortunately I do know all too well what it is like to hide." He squeezed my leg and stole a glance at me, "I forgive you."

He was quiet again for a moment, lost in thought, before whistling an exhale as he invited me into his interior world, "Whew. That was chaotic for me; to have my senses telling me one thing, and you telling me another. I hated it."

—"I'm so sorry!" I interjected.

Tim shook his head gently to let me know that wasn't what he was getting at. "Stephie, I'm realizing I did that to you for three years of our marriage. Your senses were telling you I wasn't being honest, and you were right, but I demanded you believe me instead of your gut. I'm so sorry I did that to you."

The ground felt level here. As it turns out, I was capable of creating the same chaos I had resented. There was suddenly no soapbox to stand on.

Was this real life?! I was experiencing connection with Tim in ways I had only dreamt of. I couldn't help but notice the domino effect his vulnerability was having in our marriage. It served to get my attention and inspire me to tell the truth about the coffee. Then in return, he responded with new depths of empathy and connection toward me.

Was this what it meant "to know and be known" as my tattoo in Tim's handwriting said? I brushed my fingers over the ink, now settled in my skin. I sensed Wisdom's words offer a new meaning to the phrase immortalized on my forearm. *Stephanie, this isn't something you'll ever attain completely, instead, it is the vision that pulls you into the future. This is what you seek, and to know and be deeply known by another is a lifelong pursuit.*

We all want intimacy, but we don't want it to cost us much. We want a low-risk, high-reward connection. But the truth is the path to intimacy is quite risky. Not to mention expensive. It comes at the cost of our ego. We must allow ourselves to be known in our weaknesses, shortcomings, and failures, while having the audacity to trust that Grace will receive us just as we are. We must learn to receive Love's unconditional gaze at our worst, so we may remember it was never something we had to earn in the first place.

In the creation story from the Bible, after the humans ate from the tree, God was walking through the garden in the cool of the day and asked, "Where are you?" In doing so, God was inviting Adam and Eve to come out of hiding and participate in restoration and intimacy once again. God already knew of their misstep; they weren't hiding from God as much as they were hiding from themselves; they didn't want to face what they had done. Love invited them to re-emerge and reconnect.

I was beginning to experience a miracle, one that is true for all of us. When we accept Love's invitation to emerge from our hiding—to step out of our bubbles of self-protection and be known as we are, not as we wish to be—connection in relationship has the power to transform us in ways that we cannot discover alone.

Chapter 13
Taking Responsibility

On a date with Tim, sitting on the hillside at Arrington Vineyards one summer evening, I mentioned that I'd seen Kelly Clarkson on the Today Show that morning at the gym. She was announcing she was going to be the newest coach on NBC's *The Voice*.

"Are you gonna do it?" Tim asked after taking a long sip of his red Antebellum wine, knowing full well if there was any female vocalist that could inspire me to audition, it was my girl, KC.

"Why not?" I shrugged, adding, "I think we'd be great friends, given the chance."

Tim laughed, and later told me he knew right then and there I'd be on the show.

He was right. I spent the rest of the year flying back and forth to LA and, although Kelly cried when I sang her song, "Piece by Piece," girlfriend did not turn her dang chair! She was being precious with the last slot on her team. But lucky for me, both Blake Shelton and Adam Levine did turn around, leaving me with a fun choice to make. Ultimately, I picked Adam, and enjoyed the adventure of performing two songs on a television singing competition.

Yes, in some regards, it was a dumb reality show, but in others, it was important for me to take strides in music that didn't involve Tim. Shortly after getting married, Copperlily had been our collective newlywed project. We'd toured full time for the first three years of marriage, but it had all come to a screeching halt when the mess hit the fan for us. It was an added loss for me as my marriage and music career fell apart at the same time. Somewhere along the way, I had adopted the belief that I couldn't do music without Tim. *Can you spell co·de·pen·dent?*

As the awareness dawned that I had gradually shifted to this untrue idea of only using my gifts with Tim, I accepted the responsibility for not only my talents, but also my life, dreams, and desires. They were mine, not Tim's. He was not responsible for them, I was. I knew I needed to take some action that was for me alone, to help me detach in a healthy way. *The Voice* served as something fun I could do for myself that involved my most favorite thing to do, singing. All in all, I had a great experience on the show and left a stronger singer, with some amazing new friends. But more so, I left believing I still had something to offer, and I could stand on my own two feet.

When I returned home, I found myself conflicted about running with the momentum the show had provided to build another solo music career. I had already spent the entirety of my twenties building something from the ground up, touring in a van, saying yes to every show that came my way, in an exhausting attempt at building a brand and a following. I didn't know if I had it in me to do it again at 33. One, because I didn't feel like I needed the achievement to validate my specialness or giftedness anymore, but mostly because I was noticing a growing desire to build something else: a family.

There was only one problem. My period had disappeared in the chaos of our marital undoing, and hadn't made an appearance since. By the time the dust settled from *The Voice*, it had been missing for a year and a half, and the only explanation my doctor could offer was stress, and maybe a little too much running.

Ah, running. The one thing I refused to loosen my grip on since the disclosure of Tim's secret life. As it was all unfolding, because some of the painful things that came to light in my marriage were more Tim's story to tell than mine, I wasn't sure how to let people know I was hurting without oversharing. In some twisted way, I figured if my outside wasted away, perhaps people would clue in that I was dying on the inside. I didn't feel I could talk about it publicly, but I wanted to be known in my pain, I just didn't know how. In a season when everything seemed to fall apart around me, I'd clung to something I could control: eating and exercise. At first, I could barely run a mile, but in no time, I fell in love with running. One, because it helped me blow off some anger and anxiety, and two, because I'd slimmed down quite a bit and felt powerful in my new smaller frame. I liked that people weren't commenting on my height like they had my whole life, instead they'd begun to comment on how small I was looking.

That word was like a drug: small! How foreign. I had never known what it was like to be considered physically small. I'd longed for it as I towered over my mom's petite tribe growing up — I'd even been taller than my older brother for 14 years. No, I couldn't make myself shorter, but I could make myself smaller, and I liked it.

Laura helped me see that I'd always held some resentment toward my own body, it only ignited when I was painfully reminded that there was no crying on my daddy's shoulder when the bottom fell out in my marriage. The nature of Tim's addiction had rubbed against an already raw area of my insecurities, and in some ways, being skinny felt like the middle finger I'd wanted to give my dad, and Tim, in my most hurt and abandoned moments — I just hadn't been aware of my own
motive. Sometimes the "why" behind what we do is so deep within, we must dig around in our own being to discover it. This is brave work, and we can avoid it for our whole life if we're scared enough of what we'll find. But I do believe that part of growing up, is waking up to the soul that is resiliently trying to get our attention.

I began to wonder if my body was trying to get my attention, withholding something until I was willing to look deeper? With Laura's help, I realized I had never allowed myself to grieve the rejection I'd felt from my dad. It had been within me, stored in my body, then lit like a fuse with Tim's "rejection" of me. The abandon-ment I experienced felt familiar, and it was deep. I had spent my life avoiding my grief in the name of forgiveness, afraid that if I opened that door, a dam would break that I couldn't repair. I didn't know I could grieve, hurt, and feel angry for what I didn't get as a child, while also releasing resentment, revenge, and retaliation.

Getting healthy, living whole-heartedly, and healing from the pain of living in a broken world with broken people, cannot be done all at once or overnight. New depths of healing present themselves as we progress because this is a lifelong process, and we never fully arrive or graduate from learning, growing, and awakening. Sure, things had gotten exponentially better for Tim and me, we were falling in love again, building trust and a new life together. I felt hopeful when it came to my marriage. We were out of the immediate pain of what we'd walked through, and a large part of me only wanted to look forward. I wanted to be done with "hard" forever. Hadn't I survived enough destruction? I didn't want to now survey the wreckage of my own soul. However, I was learning this new way of showing up in my own story, learning to stop asking everyone else to be responsible for my emotional well-being. Yes, my dad hadn't set me up well in childhood, and yes, my husband had let me down in my marriage, but I still had choices on how I lived my one-and-only-life and how I cared for my mind, body, and soul.

Perhaps with a new and sturdy foundation beneath me, it was time I took inventory of what I had walked through, what I had felt, and how I'd responded in my pain. Maybe it was time to face it, so I could take responsibility for how I wanted to live my life moving forward.

***

I spent the first act of my life avoiding any feelings I experienced as uncomfortable. To assist in my avoidance, I could find the silver lining in the worst of situations to distract me from pain, sorrow, fear, guilt, hurt, loneliness, or anger. It wasn't until I'd sat in Laura's office with her laminated feelings list enough times that I learned feelings are like little electrical currents the soul uses to light the path of discovery. Although they can be uncomfortable and sometimes hard to identify, in and of themself, they are neutral, neither right nor wrong, but merely informational. They serve as a little spotlight, signaling my attention in a certain direction. My feelings are also precisely that, mine. Not someone else's, so they don't need to be validated or approved of. However, because they are mine, and occur inside of me, I am responsible for what I do with them.

For me, it seemed this new disruption of longing unfulfilled—of wanting to start a family and being unable to—was acting as a guide. Maybe if I allowed myself to grieve some of the losses that I had been avoiding, and release some of the trauma that my body was apparently storing, there was something to learn.

I'd heard of Spiritual Direction from several friends and decided to enroll in a two-year Spiritual Direction program. Unbeknownst to me at the time, it would serve as another vital ingredient, alongside therapy and recovery, in my unique concoction of awakening, growth, and healing.

Spiritual Direction is the practice of being with people as they attempt to deepen their relationship with the Divine. The goal is to learn and grow in personal spirituality. It is a form of soul care given from one, to another, that helps them to pay attention to God's personal communication to him or her, to grow in intimacy with this God, and then to live out the consequences of that relationship. As I studied the practice over the course of two years, I also met with a director regularly. Sessions are a contemplative space where time seems to slow, and for a few brief moments, the noise of everyday life is held at a distance. A session is a place for honest reflection of self and listening for God — who often communicates in subtle and unexpected ways. I'd been so good at running, literally and metaphorically, it wasn't easy for me to be still at first; to listen and notice. But listening is an essential part of any conversation, so in learning to listen for God, or perhaps more so, dust for the fingerprints of God at work in my life, listening became essential.

As I learned to be honest with myself and approach God in new ways, I discovered there was no right or wrong answer to how I was feeling. There was no "how I should feel," only how I did feel, and to offer that in humility and honesty was my most sincere gift. I learned to try and not judge, analyze, or criticize what comes up in me, and that I could simply be honest, knowing God wanted to be with me just as I was. For instance, feeling anger wasn't wrong, but denying it and allowing it to become resentment or vengeance would land me in the weeds. I could bring my sincere hurt, anger, sadness, longing, joy, gratitude, pain, and loneliness to God. God could handle it.

I also realized emotions and feelings are something I experience, rather than something I am, so I didn't have to fear them. Michael Singer says, "There's nothing more important to true growth than realizing that you are not the voice of the mind, you are the one who hears it."[vii] The fact that I can observe my thoughts and feelings helps me realize they are something I have; they are not who I am.

Could it be that God already knew what had happened in my marriage, what occurred between my father and I, and how I'd felt overlooked, forgotten, and abandoned so many times in my life? That God even knew how I felt about it all, but desired for me to become aware of it? Because then, I could move through it and beyond it, instead of blindly carrying it into every area of my life.

When had I begun to believe that God would be swayed by my platitudes and fake smiles as I attempted to mask my hurt or disappointment? Probably when I was taught there were "good" and "bad" feelings, and things I "should" and "shouldn't" feel. But God is not scared of anything that could be found inside of us, and furthermore, uses the feelings, emotions, and desires within us to draw us close. I discovered that God wants to share in the revelation of awareness within me.

Nothing surprises God, and nothing scares God. But God does wait patiently for us to approach with honesty, open-mindedness, and willingness. After all, what else can we offer the One-who-knows-all? We cannot manipulate God to our limited perspective, but we can seek to better understand God's.

God has creatively given us feelings to help us navigate both the world inside, and around us. I am accountable for my actions, not my feelings. But unresolved feelings left to fester can lead to impaired behavior. That is why it is so important to acknowledge feelings, interview them, and learn from them, before we act on them.

Chip Dodd says, ``The addiction process begins in ignorance, not of a substance or an action, but the "trained ignoring" of the feelings themselves and the knowledge of what gifts they give us. Addiction is simply an impaired attempt to live fully without having to pay the price of feeling fully."[1]

Speaking of addictions, I hadn't wanted to face the truth about how much mental space running was taking up in my brain. Running made me feel safe, strong, and in control, and if exercise was good for me, then more of it was better, right? But in the parts of me I didn't let anyone see, it wasn't that I didn't want to stop, I didn't know how to stop.

I knew enough from recovery and therapy to understand it is not our vice of choice that is inherently wrong (work, shopping, booze, attention, Netflix, sex, social media, junk food, or exercise, etc.)—it is our relationship to those things that can become impaired. We can even disguise our addictions as a good thing, like serving

---

[1] Dodd, Chip. "Redefining Addiction." *Sage Hill Counseling*, 2 May 2016, https://sagehill.co/redefining-addiction/.

others, working hard, or achieving. But it is our motive and how we use them that we must be willing to be honest about. Part of the reason this whole thing can be so slippery is our relationship with our drug of choice can begin innocently and morph into trouble for us. Furthermore, our motive yesterday might be quite different from today. I think that's why it's so important to take it one day at a time and commit to a daily inventory of our own hearts, praying for the willingness to step out of hiding, isolation, and shame, and tell the truth about our struggle.

For me, the progression with eating and exercise looked something like this. At first, I was so heartbroken, I sincerely couldn't eat. It was an involuntary reaction. I began taking long walks with my dog, Riggins, to clear my head. Every once and a while, I'd jog around the neighborhood instead of punching a wall. I don't know, it felt like a healthy alternative. A few weeks after the initial blow up, I began to regain a small appetite, but I had already started feeling powerful and in control of something as I'd accidentally achieved a slight weight loss. Here is where I began to make a subtle choice, and a motive began to emerge. I didn't know if my marriage was going to make it or if Tim was going to get well, so out of fear, hurt, and anger, I decided one thing I could control was to get a sexy, revenge body in shape. That way, I'd be looking good if we got divorced, and I was thrown back into the dating pool, while simultaneously, I hoped Tim would feel the sting of regret if he decided to let me go.

That particular motive calmed down a little with recovery, but as our marriage was beginning to thrive, a new fear arose: *what if Tim only loves me now that I am smaller?* I tried to ignore it; I didn't tell anyone about this new little internal nuisance of a fear. Like a fly at a picnic, I just kept trying to swat it away. I felt imprisoned to maintain the pace I'd been keeping because I couldn't risk it all falling apart again. I knew something was going on inside of me, but I didn't want to slow down to face it. *Don't look at it, it'll go away.* I also didn't want to admit I was struggling, because that would be the first step to releasing the control I was (once again) illusioned into thinking I had.

Over time, it seemed my body eventually joined the party, begging for my attention by stopping my monthly cycle. It wasn't until my desire to grow life in my womb overshadowed my need to control, that I realized I was being invited to look at it all. Yes, some things had happened to me that hurt me and that mattered, but I was still responsible for the choices I made in response to it all. Sometimes we must thank our coping mechanisms for keeping us alive through trauma and remember to release them once the triage is over. We can release the scrappy ways we stayed alive and allow ourselves to thrive once again. For me, it was time to come out of hiding.

I began sharing about it in meetings, and I continued to unpack my resentment toward my body with Laura, who helped me choose to act lovingly toward it by nourishing it well and taking two days off from exercise a week to recover. And I invited Tim into my struggle, sharing about the insect of fear that flew around in my brain, taunting me that he'd relapse if I gained a pound. The reminder that his recovery was his responsibility — I couldn't control it, cure it, and I hadn't caused it — came as a gift. As scary as it was to open my mouth, freedom only came when I did. Connection only came once I opened myself up to it. When we isolate, we cut ourselves off from the whole, and it is no wonder we suffer. But connection is always available to us, it begins with allowing ourselves to be known amidst our struggles.

William Paul Young defines "wholeness" as "when the way of your being matches the truth of your being."[viii] Living authentically means to live congruently inwardly and outwardly. When we lie about our emotions, struggles, or motives, we also ask those closest to us to make a difficult decision: trust the words we say, or the way we live?

When people would ask if I was eating enough, my first thought would either be, "how dare they!" or "uh oh, they're on to me." Either way, my instinct was to cover up, get them off my scent. In my braver moments, I allowed myself to wonder, "When does 'getting healthy' cross over into 'becoming a problem?'" The way of my being wasn't lining up with the truth of my being, and I was beginning to experience the chaos of those things not being in alignment. It was only when I was ready to be exposed as struggling that I began to heal. I had to accept that I needed help, I couldn't find freedom in isolation. Once again, presented with the invitation to come out of the shadows, I empathized with my husband, my grandfather, and my father; all of whom had the propensity to hide. In doing so, I let them be my teachers, exhibiting how covering up and isolating in struggle didn't lead to where I wanted to go. It is surely a brave thing to let people in on our private struggles and accept help.

In our closest relationships, it can be easy to give away the responsibility to notice and care for our heart to another. But I don't believe it is the job of another to tell the truth about what is going on inside of you. When we bring ourselves just as we are, we're transformed as a result of showing up honestly. It's how we get off the bleachers, stop observing with our limited perspective, and participate in the expansion of the whole thing. Of course, we need a safe place to enter, but courage is developed in the entering, not in asking others to enter for us. Your spouse, best friend, or co-worker may try to guess what's going on inside of you—they may even pick up on some cues—but they will eventually begin to distrust you when your words don't match the energy you bring to the relationship.

You may not be surprised to learn that after practicing this integrated way of living—reconnecting and caring for my soul, mind, and body—and learning to notice and grieve some of the hurt and anger that was buried deep below my consciousness, my body responded. After three years of no cycle, I started my period again during the week of Christmas.

Could it be that our needy hearts are a gift that were always meant to point us back to the Giver? That we do not have to have it together or figured out—and neither do our loved ones—to be accepted and loved? There is no gold star for denying our fleshy hearts or struggling privately and trying to emerge again once we're "fixed." God holds it all and makes even our messes belong in the beautiful greater story somehow. All we must do is be honest with ourselves, with God, and with others, positioning ourselves as willing to see what we can't see on our own.

Curiosity is a far more fruitful teacher than defensiveness. Today when my heart feels a little chaotic, I ask myself: What happened? How do I feel about it? What do I need? Where am I off? Is there any part of this chaos I can own? How would I like to respond? Where would I like to go from here?

It seems important to mention again that we don't stay in our feelings forever. Because they are something we experience, not who we are, they do come and go. Some of us must also practice releasing them and moving through them, rather than wallowing in them for too long.

We are meant to know more as we go, not know it all before we go. God designed the process, celebrating with us as we learn, wake up, and grow into what God is already aware of.

Chapter 14
Happy Birthday Dad

My dad and I have birthdays two days apart. You'd think it would make it easy to remember, but I never once heard from my dad on my birthday. I was adamant however that he would always get a "Happy Birthday" from me, so every year I'd send a text or an email letting him know I was thinking about him, and I loved him. I didn't know who else might be celebrating him, so I never let it slide.

One year, I happened to be traveling to visit my mom in Florida on my Dad's birthday. I sat in the airport and constructed an email to him and sent it before my flight took off. For some reason it occurred to me that my brother—who had really only met and spoken to him at the funeral—might not know it was our father's birthday, so as I boarded my plane, I sent Matt a text saying, "Did you know today is Dad's birthday?" To which he quickly responded with, "No! I didn't know that. Thanks for telling me. What's his email address? I want to send him a picture of his granddaughter!" I fired off his email address, smiled at the thought of our dad seeing a picture of Ava, turned my phone on airplane mode, and took a nap in the sky.

I landed in Orlando just before lunchtime and turned on my phone to let my mom know I'd arrived. My phone danced on my thigh as it caught up on all the people who loved me enough to send me messages while I'd been traveling in the atmosphere. Ok, it was just a chatty group text of girlfriends, and my brother. It was Matt's text that caught my eye, "WHOA! He responded!"

Ooo! I thought, opening my email, *did he respond to me too?!* Apparently, I assumed the answer was going to be 'yes' because the sting of the 'no' hurt more than expected. Suddenly, I felt 14 again, standing in the back of the sanctuary at Granny's funeral as my dad shook my brother's hand, knowing his name and forgetting mine.

I let the disappointment land on me. *This sucks*, I thought to myself, *Matt didn't even know it was Dad's birthday. He wouldn't have even sent a message to be responded to if it weren't for me.* As I threw a pity party in my seat, waiting to deplane, a second thought surfaced.

True gifts are free, they don't have strings attached. If you had an expectation attached to the email you sent, it wasn't free. Was the email you sent for your dad? Or for you? If it was for your dad, let him do with it as he pleases. Perhaps the real gift you gave him today is that he got to hear from his estranged son and see a picture of his granddaughter for the first time. Damn this getting healthy stuff. It was a new perspective, and it felt true. I wanted to reach for it as it danced before me—like a balloon blowing in the wind—and I wanted to hold it, but I also wanted to feel sorry for myself.

Then, still sitting in my Southwest seat waiting, came another whisper in my consciousness. *Both are true, it's sad you didn't get what you wanted from your dad. There's space for you to feel that sadness, but don't ask your brother or father to hold that for you today. Sometimes love is quiet and unacknowledged. Trust that you played a part in a special gift to your dad. You're not alone though. Who is someone safe you can invite in to witness your disappointment?*

I opened my texts again and chose my favorite person, Tim. He knew better than anyone this love I had for my dad, and my desire to be loved in return. Tim had walked alongside so much of my personal and relational healing in this department, he didn't need context or explanation to understand the disappointment I was experiencing. I typed ferociously:

"I told Matt today was our dad's birthday, he didn't know, and asked for his email address. I gave it to him, and apparently Dad responded to him already, but I haven't gotten a response, or a Happy Birthday for my now belated birthday! Feeling sad and overlooked. Just wanted someone to know. Love youuuu."

Send.

I took a deep breath, got off the plane, and found Mommy in the passenger pickup area. With it being lunchtime, and both of us loving food, it was clear what our first order of business was. We drove to a cute little seafood place on the water, catching up and enjoying the beginning of our mommy-daughter day together. I was grateful for the distraction but couldn't help noticing Tim had not responded yet. *Grace, grace, grace,* I coached myself privately. *Maybe it was a busy day at work.*

We had to wait for our table, so we walked along a pier, looked at turtles and birds. Mommy told me about her new therapist, Pamela. I was so grateful she was beginning to unpack some of her own story. Sitting down at our table, she told me there were things she wanted to tell me but wasn't ready yet. I told her that I was proud of her for continuing to grow, and I would love to hear anything she wanted to share when she was ready. It was a deep conversation, and I didn't want to complicate it by talking about my dad—as we had very different relationships with him.

Holding this space for my mom, and grace for my dad and brother, and now Tim—who still hadn't responded—was clearly presenting itself to be a growth opportunity for me. I could feel my little balloon of fresh perspective that had visited me earlier getting tossed in the wind. But I also wanted to practice this new way of showing up in my own life. I tried to remind myself that there was enough for me, I have not been forgotten, and I am also allowed to need. If I am willing to detach from *how* my needs are met, then I am available to be surprised when the answer arrives.

Great speech healthy self, I thought sarcastically, wrestling internally because I didn't want to detach from Tim meeting my needs yet. I had already unconsciously decided that today it was exclusively his responsibility. After all, he was my husband for crying out loud, hadn't he taken vows or something? *Show your wife some love dude!*

What do I have to do to get a response here? Light myself on fire?! I thought as I fumed over Tim not caring enough about me to even text back yet, let alone CALL! I could feel I was giving into another pity party, so I took a few deep breaths.

Were you confident in Tim's love when he kissed you goodbye at the airport this morning? The question bubbled up; I was getting better at listening.

Hmm. Yes. I responded, interested by the question, and feeling myself soften as another followed on its heels.

Is it likely that he changed his mind in the past few hours, that he is suddenly no longer for you, but now, in fact, is against you — and this is how he has decided to let you know? Or could it be that you don't know the whole story yet?

I knew Tim was in my corner. And if he was being uncaring, I knew I could address that, but it was unlikely. *What is wanted and needed? What are you looking for?* Another question, leading me to my own self-discovery.

Connection. I realized my deeper desire was to be known in this loneliness. Of course, I wanted it to come from Tim, there is a redemptive storyline I am always drawn to, where he will be everything to me my dad couldn't be — but as poetic as that is, it's a set up for disappointment for both of us to always expect it to play out that way. Part of the beauty of marriage is that we're in it for the long haul. I will always return to Tim, but he cannot bear the weight of being my only source of connection for a lifetime. When I find connection in a healthy way elsewhere, the one Tim and I have is only deepened when I later share it with him.

I excused myself from the table with Mommy. Sitting in a bathroom stall, I texted my sweet friend, Lindsey Frazier — someone who knew enough of my life and history to understand the context of my disappointment — and immediately received a loving and affirming response from her. She empathized with my hurt and agreed that it was a gift for my dad to hear from his son and affirmed that I had served as a bridge between them, and I was naturally feeling the stretch. I exhaled, feeling relief, as if the knot in my chest was loosening. When our experience is witnessed by another, we are reminded that we are seen, loved, and held. There is space for us. We all need this gift. It's how we live in the paradox that life is tragic, and God is faithful.

It wasn't long after that my phone rang; it was Tim. It had been two hours since I texted him and this was the first peep I was hearing out of him. We small-talked for a little while, and I waited for him to address my text, but it didn't come.

Feeling like my growing anger might come out sideways if I let it fester any longer, I took a deep breath and centered myself before I spoke again.

What are you looking for from him? Connection. I reminded myself to invite, stay curious, don't get big or small, stand my sacred ground.

"Hey Timmy, did you get my text earlier?" I asked, careful to keep daggers out of my tone.

"Oh crap!" he said with sincerity. "I saw something came in from you earlier, but I haven't even looked at it yet," his voice grew distant as he pulled the phone away from his face to read the text. "It was a CRAZY morning here; both of my bosses were out, and I was doing three people's jobs today!" he added. "Hold on, reading it now."

I felt my heart soften as I stayed quiet, letting him catch up, regaining hope that he could join me in the place I'd desired all along. I knew his job as an assistant producer for a live radio show was chaotic. His lack of response made a lot more sense.

"Oh Steph. I'm so sorry. It really sucks that you didn't get a response from your dad. Have you checked again?" he asked almost optimistically, as though maybe I had forgotten to refresh my inbox every few minutes. Then he added a thought, seemingly as it occurred to him, "Oh man, I can only imagine that must have been so lonely not hearing from me after sending that a few hours ago, tell me what that was like for you."

Yes, he actually asks me questions like that. What a gift he is. It was delayed, it didn't come at the exact moment I wanted it, and I had to be patient and trust others were for me, as opposed to against me. But it wasn't lost on me that here it was, the very thing I had desired: connection, intimacy, and to be known. It also occurred to me that if I would have acted out of fear, insecurity, or judgment, and approached Tim in the height of my hurt and anger with guns a-blazing, this gentle and generous connection I was experiencing would have eluded me. We participate in every experience we have, even if it's just the story we choose to believe.

I never did hear from my dad that day. I reached out again around Father's Day, then again around Christmas, but still no response. While he never initiated contact, my efforts to connect with him were also sparse in this season because I needed my own space to grieve some of our shared story. I had accepted that he couldn't father me in the way I deserved or wanted. But I didn't have a lot of emotional reserves as I was learning to hold space for the little girl that didn't have her dad around when she was growing up, the little girl who had quietly been haunted by the fear she would always have to be the pursuer to receive love. I hadn't realized that I could be gracious to my dad and compassionate to his side of the story while also honoring mine. I had always just abandoned my childhood perspective or denied it, until I realized I was living out of it still as an adult, and that hadn't done me any favors.

Somehow, there was enough space in the Universe for both my dad's perspective and my own— and both mattered. I could reclaim my sacred ground and let myself be loved.

Chapter 15
An 8-Hour Drive for Breakfast

A new question surfaced for me about a year after the birthday ghosting from my dad. *If you were to get the phone call that your dad was gone today, would you be at peace with your efforts to know him and love him?*

The tone of the question was curious, thought-provoking, and not at all judgmental. I sensed there was no right or wrong answer, the question itself seemed to be the point, inviting me to take a personal inventory of where I stood with my dad. I thought about the question for a while, carrying it with me for a few days. It almost felt like a premonition, how much longer did I have with him?

It wasn't uncommon for people to mention how gracious they thought I was toward my dad. I'd spent a lot of my twenties on stage telling the dramatic story of meeting him at a funeral and how the first words he spoke to me were calling me the wrong name. I preached forgiveness and love from a young girl's perspective, I even wrote a book about it back then—a premature attempt at telling our story before it was ready to be shared. But as I sat with this new question, I knew there was more to our story. I knew there were new levels of knowing and loving him. I knew loving him also meant trying to understand his experience better, and not just defending mine.

The energy I had brought to our dynamic had always been fragranced with an aroma of "daddy-do-you-see-me?!" Granted, it was stronger at times than others, but it had always been there, nonetheless.

As I had been practicing living out of the love, belonging, and value that I now understood had always been mine, I noticed a new curiosity arising about my dad as a person. There was so much I didn't know about him. What was he like as a little boy? As a high school or college student? What had the past 30 years of isolation been like for him? What did he know today that he didn't know last year? What was he good at? What had his experience as a human on Earth been like?

Clearly, functioning in the world was hard for him. The constant shame he carried for not "doing more" with his life, or not finding enough victory from his mental illness was already so dominant, so heavy. At times he'd experience a small victory and feel encouraged, then his brain would imbalance, stunting his progress and derailing him. By the time he'd balance back out, discouragement would paralyze him as shame criticized his loss of momentum. He would perceive it as "back to square one" and forward motion felt too daunting at that point, so he just continued to shut himself off from the world.

After 60-some years of this pattern, I had to assume he would be growing weary, and I was in a place in my life where I could offer a more generous perspective to him. I could see that every time he ventured out of his self-imposed isolation to respond to me or — on the rare occasion — see me, he was exercising every ounce of bravery he could muster. Had I ever been grateful for that offering, or had I only criticized it because I wanted more?

I wondered how he had experienced me in our previous encounters. Yes, I needed to grieve that I was once a little girl that didn't get what she deserved or needed but wasn't it true that my dad had also been a little boy once who didn't get what he needed? He wasn't a bad man because he didn't have what I was looking for. Had he sensed my hunger for him to love me, and it only overwhelmed him? Intensifying the feedback loop he already played in his chaotic mind — frustrating him that the world seemed to take more than he was able to offer? Did my insatiable desire for more translate to him that he would never be enough? And possibly perpetuate his hiding?

I wanted to try again — with whatever time we might have left — now with a new understanding of my belonging and significance in this world, untethered from him. I was confident enough of my beloved-ness that I sincerely didn't feel like I needed anything from my dad, I simply desired to know him. I wanted to be a gift to him, without strings attached. I was free to love him as he was, not as I wanted him to be.

I knew engaging him was risky, not only because of the potential of disappointment that may come from his silence, but also the tornado of emotion that might come with his response. I wasn't naive or foolish, I'd experienced chaos with him before. Sometimes what he said was strange, painful, or difficult to understand. Sometimes it was sound and solid. Sometimes there was no response at all. But I knew I had the tools and resources to help me sort through whatever might come up. My worth was not on the line here, neither was his. I could face whatever outcome presented itself.

After mulling it over, I answered the question that had arisen within me with confidence. *No. I don't think I would be at peace if he were gone today, I haven't done all I can; I have more in me to give.*

The problem was he hadn't responded to any of my texts or emails in two years.

I'd reached out several times before and after the birthday ghosting, and still, no response. But maybe there was something else going on? Maybe it wasn't that he didn't love me or want to respond. Maybe he just couldn't. What else was possible?

The thought dawned on me how much my dad had liked Tim. They had met once at a Cracker Barrel on I-40. We'd been driving home from a tour that finished in Oklahoma, and I noticed we'd be passing an hour south of where Dad lived. I impulsively wrote to him the night before we planned to pass through (sound familiar?), and to my surprise, he agreed to meet us. He'd raved at what a "winner, winner, chicken dinner" Tim was in several texts over the next year before disappearing again. I could tell there was something about Tim's gentle nature that had put my dad and his social anxieties at ease, coaxing him out of his shell ever so slightly.

It had been four years since that encounter. It was the last I'd seen him, and he'd gone silent again shortly after. I remember standing behind him in the cashier's line, waiting to pay. Tim had excused himself to use the restroom, and although I needed to pee so badly, I couldn't tear myself away from my dad's enormous presence. The meal was over, and we were about to go our separate ways again for who-knew-how-long. I could feel myself hoarding the precious last few moments of being in his presence. I loved standing near him, I felt so small next to his large, tall frame — it felt indulgent. I understood my own frame better in the context of his. I could pee anytime; I wasn't willing to sacrifice even a second of our last few moments together.

I knew he didn't have Tim's phone number, so I began scheming. (Side note: once I notice I'm scheming, I try to bring someone else into my "best thinking." Sometimes it is, in fact, brilliant, and sometimes it needs a little tweaking). I decided to invite Tim into my scheme and asked if he would feel comfortable reaching out to my dad and seeing if he could get ahold of him. I didn't want to use Tim, or be sneaky with my dad, but I did care about my father's well-being, and I wanted to see him again. I couldn't shake the feeling that I didn't have much time left.

Our dear friends, Gavin and Cait, had recently moved to Arkansas. They're the kind of people who ruin neighbors for you forever because no one will ever compare. *Sorry new neighbors, it is what it is.* When I asked for their new address, I couldn't believe it was only three miles from my dad's house. My plan was this: if Tim or I could just make contact with my dad, we could coordinate a visit with our old neighbors and see my dad too. Knowing he spooked easily, it would be much less pressure for him if we 'happened to be in the area,' rather than him feel he had to host us, entertain us, or shoulder the whole purpose of a visit. We would stay with friends, and just offer to take him out for a meal. *Easy. Great plan.*

I waited patiently as Tim took every bit of the day to think about my request. Coaching myself: *leave room for yes, no, or maybe. Let him decide, don't manipulate. Be open-handed with the outcome. If your motive is love, you can trust the process.* When I couldn't take it anymore, I asked Tim if he'd landed anywhere, or if he needed more time.

He told me he was nervous to call, but he was open to it. We looked at our calendar, agreed on a weekend with Gavin and Cait to go visit, and Tim dialed my dad's number — putting it on speaker phone so I could listen in.

It rang, rang, rang, rang. Until a generic, robotic voicemail asked him to leave a message.

Tim, a classic phone pacer, frantically walked around the living room as he put on his "phone voice," speaking to the voicemail, and I followed behind him like a puppy.

"Hey Scott! This is Tim Skipper, Stephanie's husband. We met a couple years ago at Cracker Barrel. Hey, uh, we are planning a trip to Arkansas soon to visit some friends that just moved out there, and we wondered if you'd be up for another meal together? We'd love to get together while we're close by. Yeah, just ah, well, hope to see you and catch up. Let me know if this is something you're interested in. Hope you're well."

Tim hung up and exhaled. "I was so nervous," he said with a boyish smile.

"Me too!" I said, grateful he was willing to join me in trying to love my dad.

Not long after, Tim's phone buzzed with a text. "He responded!" Tim gasped as he read it out loud: "Hey Skip! Got your call. I am open to this. I think it's time."

"He's ALIVE!" I said, only partially hyperbolic. The plan was coming together, but in no way secure. We would make our way to Arkansas in a little over two weeks, and that was plenty of time for Dad to spook or go rogue. *Hold it loosely*, I reminded myself. *Today, he knows you want to see him, let that be the gift you offer for now. We will see what comes when it comes.*

***

The drive was close to eight hours from Nashville to Rogers, Arkansas. We left on a Friday afternoon after Tim got off work, looking forward to one of Gavin's promised gourmet meals that would be waiting for us when we arrived later that night. We had plans to meet my dad the next morning for breakfast, location and time still TBD. As we drove, I verbally processed with Tim, my captive audience and sounding board.

"I looked up a couple brunch spots, there's one called 'The Buttered Biscuit' that looks cute. Maybe I'll suggest that as a meeting place?" I was scanning the hipster-influenced, avocado toast-inspired menu as I spoke—I love anticipating a good meal, it's part of the experience for me—but Tim responded with silence.

"Can I make a suggestion?" he eventually said cautiously, obviously treading lightly, which annoyed me. *Why was he handling me with kid gloves? I was being very mature about this.*

"Okay…" I said, wondering what sort of 'Tim insight' he was about to drop on me.

"Do you think your dad will feel comfortable in a trendy place like that?" he asked.

I was mad. I already felt like I was giving up so much, extending so far to try and reach my dad. I was literally driving eight hours and giving up a weekend for a MEAL with him, couldn't I at least have the meal I wanted?!

My eyes filled with tears, I knew his question was warranted, but I didn't want to entertain it yet. I wanted my dad to ask me what I wanted, I wanted him to invite *me* to brunch, I wanted him to drive the equivalent of a workday to see me. My inner child, still looking for her daddy to delight in her, was presently in control of my person. I felt deeply in touch with that younger part of myself, and she was hurt. She was angry. She also felt a small hissy fit was warranted.

I told Tim what was going on inside of me. I've said it before, I'll say it again, something shifts when we put words to what feels chaotic inside. Obviously, it's important to select a safe and trustworthy person, but articulating our inner experience sheds new light, offers new perspective, and takes humility. It means we are willing to be exposed in our process. It means we haven't arrived yet and we need something. Perspective, insight, peace, grace, understanding, wisdom, love, strength, hope—these things are available to all of us, and we position ourselves in a way to receive them when we tell the truth about our hearts.

Once I let the little girl in me have the microphone for a moment, with my trusted and captive audience, I felt calmer. I was able to regulate and remember that asking my dad to give me something he didn't have to give was not only disappointing to me, but it also wasn't loving towards him. My dad was sick, and sick people act sick. I wouldn't ask someone with Covid to run a marathon with me. I had learned to differentiate that his lack of emotional availability did not have to equal my lack of deserving it. All his handicap meant towards me was that he was not a wise place to be looking for what I wanted and needed.

Of course, I had to grieve that he didn't have the emotional maturity to father me. It's natural for a little girl to want her daddy to care for her—even at 35. So, for a brief moment, driving west on I-40, I had to acknowledge it again as reality, feel what it brought up, grieve it, and release it. To accept that he didn't have it was painful, because I deeply wanted him to have it, or at least go find it! But I wasn't responsible for him, I was responsible for me. I had choices on how to deal with my disappointment. I could deny that I wanted anything from him (or anyone else), cynically assuming I just got the short end of the stick. I could live as a victim and make everyone pay for what my dad didn't give me. Or I could ask my Higher Power for what I was looking for and trust that it was available to me—I might just be surprised by the form it arrived in. I could dare to believe that I was worth being cared for and loved well, that there was enough for me. I had tasted the freedom that came with detaching from HOW my needs were going to be met and living in the active faith that what is needed will always make its way to me, especially when I am open to it.

I felt myself level out as we drove and was able to remember the purpose of this trip: to know my dad. To meet him in his world, to invite him to move an inch instead of expecting a mile. I tried on a lens from his perspective and thought about how brave it was that he'd even responded to us. It was a gift that he'd even said yes to meeting at all. We'd only met in person a handful of times, and I recalled him telling me he'd been awake all night, vomiting, because he was so nervous to see me. He was offering everything he had to give.

I returned to wanting to know about his human experience. I hoped he would tell me about his childhood, his college years, his life in general. While he was still here, I wanted to know: what was it like to be Scott Smith? I knew if those were my questions, the chances of him opening up were more likely if he was in an environment that felt safe to him. And this 6'5", 300-pound, Southern boy, and former trucker who favored overalls, may not feel at home in a small, custom-built, reclaimed wood, hipster booth. Not to mention a menu he wouldn't know how to interpret.

Tim chimed in again and said, "What if you asked him if he knew of any places we could go?"

That seemed reasonable. I began constructing a text to my dad from my phone, taking over correspondence from Tim, who was driving.

To my pleasure, he responded relatively quickly! The plan was still a go! We agreed on a time and my dad did, in fact, have a suggestion as to where we should dine… The Village Inn.

"Hmm, what's the Village Inn?" I wondered out loud, assuming it was probably a local mom-and-pop place.

Tim laughed as he interjected, "He suggested the Village Inn?! Ha! That's awesome. I'm so glad we asked him to pick the place. Yeah, that makes perfect sense—of course, he chose Village Inn, he drove trucks for 15 years!"

Tim seemed to know something I didn't, so this time I directed my question to him, "What's the Village Inn?"

"You've never seen a Village Inn? Think: a step below Denny's. Just cheap, greasy, diner food. It'll be great."

"NOOOO I WANT MY BOUJEE BISCUIT!" I lamented in jest. We both laughed because what else was there to do? Village Inn it was.

***

The next morning, my spidey-senses said Dad was there as we parked and approached the restaurant. I was nervous and excited. Tim opened the door, and I stepped into the entryway, spotting my dad sitting on a vinyl bench in the lobby, waiting for us. His face brightened when he saw me, and he began the slow process of standing up to greet us. He looked older, moving slower, and—as predicted—was wearing tattered overalls, cut off at the hem. His ankles showed as he was seated, wearing slip-on shoes on sockless feet. A camel-colored, zip-up hoodie, insulated with a fabric resembling long underwear, hung open on his large frame. The arm cuffs were cut off haphazardly, like a toddler had done it with kitchen shears, leaving the sleeves to rest at three quarter length down his long arm. His hair was grayer than I remembered, but his glasses were thick and sliding down his nose, just as I remembered. This was him put together. My heart softened, and I felt strangely responsible to protect him, to put him at ease, as I could feel his uncertainty about how to proceed.

This is so brave of him, I thought to myself, receiving the seemingly small gesture he was offering by being here as the monumental one it was. *He really loves me.*

The hostess sat us at a table in the middle of the busy restaurant, Tim sat next to me, and my dad sat across from me. We scanned our menus and made small talk as we settled into what would be our shared space together for the next two hours.

The conversation ping-ponged all over the place. I told him how I'd been a contestant on *The Price Is Right* and *Let's Make a Deal*, not winning on either show but enjoying the experience, nonetheless. I did not mention my most recent TV appearance, however. I don't know, I felt like it might be a bit of a buzzkill to bring up that I'd recently been on NBC's *The Voice*, singing a Kelly Clarkson song about her absent father. Instead, I navigated around that one by telling him how I'd appeared on every one of our local news stations after finding a now-convicted rapist hiding from police under our crawl space—that's always a good ice breaker, and likely a story for another book.

My dad was a walking paradox. Seemingly as simple as they come, yet more complicated than I could explain. He loved to think, learn, and research, favoring his studies with certain televangelists and fire-and-brimstone pastors, yet in many ways he was like a stunted adolescent boy who filled his time with video games and TV shows.

He told us of a little dog he'd taken in named Sarah. She'd been abused by some teenage boys, and it had taken him two weeks to earn her trust. She'd hidden under his coffee table, refusing to come out, growling and barking if he tried to approach. But he had been gentle and patient with her, eventually luring her out with treats, and now they were inseparable. I showed him a picture of Riggins, our beloved pitbull, and casually mentioned that he would love to meet Sarah.

"You're welcome to visit us in Nashville anytime, Dad, we'd

love to have you and little Sarah."

At one point, he ventured into the topic of flat-earth conspiracy, speaking with confidence as though he assumed we would agree with his perspective. When he observed us not affirming with head nods and contributions to the theory, he stopped himself mid-sentence and questioned both Tim and I, "Are either of you familiar with flat-earth research?" He let the question land, looking over his glasses and shifting his eyes between us.

"Oh, I'm familiar with it," Tim offered, being a bit of a conspiracy theory aficionado himself, "I just don't know that I buy — "

"Oooookay," Dad interrupted, pushing his glasses back up his nose, "That's okay, you're not there yet. Alright. I thought you might be, okay." His tone was simultaneously gentle and conciliatory, like he was sure he knew something we didn't, and it was only a matter of time until we discovered it for ourselves. He took a huge bite of his overly buttered pancake and clammed up.

I changed topics and brought up my brother, Matt. Dad finished his bite and re-engaged. "Yeah, he sent me an email with a picture of his little girl a while back, sweet lil' thing. I told him she was gonna need a little brother soon." He smiled, appearing to think that was pretty clever, or perhaps recalling a moment that he deeply treasured — receiving an email from his son offering an olive branch.

"When do you think y'all will start a family, it's probably about time don't you think?" Dad asked me, completely unaware of our current infertile situation. Our desire to be parents was growing every day. But at this point, it had been over two years, and there was still no sign of my period.

Grace, grace, grace, I thought to myself as I answered honestly. "We can't wait to be parents; we've been trying for a while now, but it's proving to be a little complicated for us."

My dad turned his head to the side and said, "Aw-kay, now what does that mean?" I knew my dad had an innocence about him, I also knew that in his experience, babies came easily. I had been a surprise that arrived unexpectedly, and my parents hadn't had to spend any time trying for my brother. Apparently, I was really going to have to spell this out for him.

"I haven't had a period in over two years," I told him bluntly. He didn't seem uncomfortable. I assured him we were looking into it, and I was grateful the conversation moved on.

Close to an hour into our time together, it was obvious everyone was feeling more comfortable. The coffees had been refilled, our bellies were stuffed, and the four year's worth of ice that had accumulated since we'd last seen each other, had been broken. My dad spoke faster now, perhaps because of the caffeine, perhaps because he'd acclimated to his environment, but it almost seemed as if he had some things he needed to say and wanted me to understand.

"The Lord revealed something to me a few years ago, and it made a lot of sense." He spoke authoritatively, convinced of what he was preparing to share.

This could go in any direction, I thought, knowing from experience that sometimes he spoke in nonsense, other times, he pulled from a deep insight and wisdom—he was a true wild card.

Continuing on, he spoke of a traumatic event I'd never heard of before. "My mother suffered from Paranoid Schizophrenia, and one time she was naked and outside in front of the neighbors. I had to tackle her in the front yard just to get her back in the house. She favored Steve, my little brother, but I was bigger, so when she had an episode, I was the one who had to wrestle her to the ground. I was just a teenager. Anyway, the Lord used one of these scenarios to speak to me." He paused and looked up from the table to make sure I was with him still.

I nodded, as if to say, *Please, continue!*

"Well," he began again, "The Lord took me back in my spirit to when she was charging towards me, not in her right mind, with a butcher knife in her hand. I was cornered in the kitchen, and I was terrified. If I moved to the right, I was within her reach, and to the left, I was within her reach, so in that moment—I hid within myself. The Lord said to me, 'Scott, from this point on, you grew in age and stature, but emotionally, you were stunted.'"

I was shocked at how insightful this was, that aligned with my experience of him for sure. His self-awareness was remarkable. He went on to share how in his stuntedness, marriage had been a bad idea, and he didn't blame my mom at all for leaving, he understood how the situation was too much for her — too much for anyone.

I wanted to stay here for a moment. But I knew better than to make a big deal about this treasure he was bestowing upon me. My dad was like a traumatized animal, something seemingly insignificant could trigger him at any point, causing him to retreat again within. I didn't want him to feel patronized and shut down, so I made a mental note to borrow Tim's elephant recall later when we could speak candidly about all of this, because the tender moment was short-lived. Dad moved on quickly to a narrative he'd created to make sense of his own life.

"See, I was never supposed to get married. I was supposed to be a single man and go into the ministry. I got distracted when I met your mother, and that's where I got off track."

Yes, yes, I've heard this before, I thought to myself as I let him talk about how he "missed it" or "blew it" at several specific moments he'd identified. One being after the divorce, he believed he'd stayed 13 years longer than he was "supposed to" in trucking. "I missed it again," he commented on his own story as if it had always been fixed as opposed to fluid. "It set me even further back," he continued. "Yeah, I dug my hole even deeper back then. And I just haven't been able to crawl out."

I listened to him speak as though he'd cracked the code on how he'd become a failure. His world was black and white, filled with "supposed to" and absolutes. As a result, his shame was palpable. He'd combed through his past so many times in isolation, looking for signs of where he may have gotten off, why his life had become what it was, and how it was possible he wasn't further along on a path to healing. It was as if he was trying to organize the chaos inside of himself, and he'd arrived at a few storylines that worked for him.

I wished he could see how it was his isolation and attempts to fix himself privately, only believing he could emerge once he was eventually perfect, that had kept him sick. We all fall off the path, misstep, or realize we've stayed too long in a season we need to get out of. Healing is never linear. He wasn't alone in having struggles and shortcomings, he was more a part of something than he was separate from it—namely, the imperfect human race. Rather, he viewed his brokenness as superiorly impaired, a forever blemish on his misguided goal of perfection.

As I listened to him to speak in absolutes about pivotal moments in his path, he surprised me with a curveball I hadn't heard before.

"But I was NEVER supposed to have children," he said with conviction, re-engaging my attention.

That stung a little. I wasn't sure why he thought that was something I, his child, needed to know. I felt the inclination to receive that comment as a new rejection from him, to nurse it, absorb it, take it personally, and feel sorry for myself. But instead, I chose to remember that he was telling me about himself, not about me. I knew, on the deepest level, that something bigger than both my mother and father wanted me here, and for reasons beyond my understanding, that Higher Power chose to bring me forth using this man. I knew I had choices as to how I responded to his statement. I also knew that I didn't just have to absorb it or take it on as a personal criticism. I had been practicing finding and using my voice, and this moment felt like an opportunity to exercise it. *Say what you mean. Mean what you say. Don't say it mean.*

"That's an interesting statement." I said, gently interrupting his monologue. "How do you reconcile Matt and me then?" I asked sincerely, intentionally selecting my tone to be curious, as opposed to accusatory.

He didn't miss a beat, "Well, I believe there are a certain number of souls and God just assigns them into bodies."

Treading lightly, I decided to offer some of my perspective here. "With all due respect Dad, I am going to push back here just a little bit, is that okay?" I said with a smile. He knew I was feisty, and I think he liked it.

"Okay," he said with a smirk as he relaxed back in his chair and folded his three-quarter length covered arms across his large belly.

"One thing I'm learning as we deal with infertility is: I am powerless to create life in my womb. I can give it every best shot, but I can't make it happen if God doesn't breathe life into what Tim and I are bringing to the table. You're saying you weren't supposed to be a parent, but you didn't just "make it happen" by having sex. Just because someone has sex, doesn't mean they will be parents. You said it yourself, God is the one who releases the soul and gives the life. Apparently, He chose YOU to participate in bringing ME into the world, and well…" I made sure he was looking at me as I added a smirk for levity, "I like being here."

"Well…" he paused and smiled, "Okay, you got me there," he stuttered, seemingly trying to decide where to go from this point. Then he laughed and said, "Yeah, okay. I'm gonna have to think about that one some more."

I had so much compassion for this man. It's as though I could see his true self, his inner God-ordained self, through all his baggage, confusion, mental illness, isolation, and insecurity—he was in there, and it was easy for me to see him and love him. I wished he would let himself out of the prison of his own perspective and see that marriage, parenthood, career struggles, baggage from family of origin, even mental illness, are not things we are meant to master. Rather, they are invitations that reveal the areas we still need to grow, change, and heal, if we are only willing.

Finishing breakfast, he excused himself to use the restroom after we paid the check, and a few moments later he joined us outside in the Village Inn parking lot to say our goodbyes. Knowing from past experiences he didn't care much for physical touch, I asked permission before going in to hug him. He answered with an awkward shrug-of-the-shoulders and a simple, "I guess so."

"This was great, Dad," I said as I stepped out of his clumsy almost-embrace. "Thank you for meeting up with us. How about we let this visit settle in, and I'll circle back in a week or two and check on you? I'll ask you then how you're feeling about making a visit to us in Nashville?"

I barely had the words out as he interrupted, "Naw, I already decided I'm gonna do it. Yeah, I just made the decision when I was in the bathroom."

I smiled, noticing the effort he was making, and I was grateful he was keeping the door open to further connection. I didn't know if anything would come from it, but for this day, he was saying yes.

Chapter 16
The Visit

Dad and I had never spent more than two consecutive hours together, and it was usually in a neutral, public place, like a restaurant. The idea of him coming for three days to stay in my house was both exciting and terrifying. Once I returned home from the quick trip to Arkansas, I held his "yes" loosely, but within ten days of my return, we agreed he would come visit the last weekend in April. As the plans were finalized, we agreed that to make the drive worth it for him, he'd come Friday evening and leave Monday morning. I told him he could plan to arrive any time after 5 p.m. on Friday, because I worked until 4 p.m. He sent a thumbs up emoji, and I didn't hear anything more from him in the weeks leading up to his trip.

When the day came for him to visit, Tim and I were both nervous enough to slip out of work early. I was vacuuming the stairs around 3:30 p.m., musing that I didn't know if he'd even show, or what he liked to do, or if he drank alcohol, or how we were going to fill nearly three days together, when suddenly Tim yelled over the vacuum, "HE'S HERE!"

I got to the door in time to watch him struggle to remove his large frame from his little, single cab GMC Canyon, parked on the street in front of my house. I met him, and his Maltese mix, Sarah, in the front yard. Sarah was clearly possessive of Dad. As I approached, she positioned herself in front of him while her abrasive yaps assaulted my ears. I moved to greet Dad, but he cringed and retreated away from me, like a wounded animal himself, before I could even touch him.

"Be careful now!" he said, grabbing his ribcage, "I took a spill the other day walking Sarah, I wasn't even sure if I was going to make this trip." He lifted his left arm to reveal an oozing open wound just below his forearm, a result of his 6'5", 310-pound frame colliding with the asphalt. "I may have cracked a rib or two, it took me 30 minutes to get back on my feet—knocked the wind out of me pretty good—but I wasn't gonna miss this; naw, I decided I was still gonna come, this visit was long overdue."

Concerned, but grateful he still made the trip, I helped him in the house and showed him to his room, then we sat outside for a while and enjoyed the spring evening while the dogs played in the yard. Although it was unspoken, I think we both realized quickly that the pups were a nice buffer for the occasional awkward moments between us humans—giving us something to direct our attention toward when the complicated nature of our relationship seemed too overwhelming to face directly.

Eventually, we decided to take the dogs with us to dinner, so we moved our reunion to the patio of Edly's BBQ in Sylvan Park. Tim offered to go inside and order for all of us while Dad and I sat together outside with the dogs, and he tried his hand at small talk.

"What do you usually get here?" he asked, keeping his eyes on his menu even though he'd already told Tim his order.

"I usually get the turkey plate," I responded, before feeling the need to offer, "it's a little lighter."

"Well now, I was gonna say!" Dad said with gumption, barely letting me finish my sentence. Noticing his own enthusiasm, he settled down and tried to collect his words. "Okay," he restarted with his southern drawl, "you're a lot thinner than the last time I saw you a few years ago. I guess what I'm trying to say is... you don't need to mess with perfection... So don't lose any more?" His tone raised, finishing his thought like a question. Glancing up at me briefly to see if it was okay that he'd given his opinion.

My insides became a puddle of goo. I felt a warmth reach a depth within me that I didn't know existed; like a balm filling cracks I wasn't even aware of. My father, in his own way, had just told me I was beautiful. To the best of his ability, he told me I was perfect just the way I was—even as he tripped over his words a bit, and it felt as though it was important to him that he say it. In that moment, I felt something in me begin to heal.

What a gift. In a season where I was reconciling my animosity toward my body, a redemptive moment revealed itself. I'd learned to trust that the care and affirmation I desired from my dad would come to me in other healthy ways, and it had. There was no scarcity of love and belonging with God. But my commitment to my dad was to simply meet him where he was and love him as he was, releasing him from the expectation of being able to "father" me. However, much to my surprise, in his own way, Dad had done just that. He blessed the body I had wanted to reject for so long. It was an unexpected gift, coming from the mouth of the man I'd craved it from the most. The moment was short but reverent. We moved on to other small talk, but I savored his words privately and made a place for them within me.

After dinner, we swung by a CVS to get some gauze and bandages for his road-burned forearm. When we got back to the house, I asked him if I could help him with it. To my surprise, he agreed. We stood in my small, 1960's guest bathroom, as I quietly delighted in the close physical proximity he was allowing me. I gently dressed his oozing arm with Neosporin, then placed a piece of gauze over it, and finally wrapped it in an ACE bandage. It was an intimate and tender moment. Here I was, tending to the wounds of the man who had arguably wounded me most deeply, and it was my joy to do so. I wanted him to know he was worth caring for. The moment also felt like a metaphor. He'd not even given his physical ailments a second thought, driving eight hours with a cracked rib and bleeding arm. It felt symbolic of how he'd tended to his whole life, wounded young, then emotionally limping through the rest of his life, hoping it would just get better if he waited long enough.

The next morning, I made a Chemex — *no, there was no coconut in it* — and offered some to Dad. He finished the cup in no time, and I offered to grind up some more beans and make another pour-over.

"Do you have any instant coffee?" he asked, subtly reminding me he was still a trucker at heart. I had some that was close to expiring that I'd used once in a brownie recipe and offered to keep it at the kitchenette in the basement where he was staying. I showed him how to use the electric water kettle, and it blew his mind. He ordered one online that same day so it would be waiting for him when he got home.

In our limited communication leading up to this visit, I'd mentioned we could take the dogs on a walk, so over coffee I asked if he felt up for it.

"Aw yeah, I'll be alright. I didn't want to miss out, so I bought a walking stick, and it arrived the day before I left," he said with a boyish smirk, obviously feeling proud of himself. "Not too long of one though—and I'm not gonna bring Sarah. Let's just take Regis... Regan? Uh. What's his name again?"

"It's Riggins" I said, smiling inside as I noticed the gift in his slip of the tongue. It hadn't been personal when I met him at 14, and he'd called me "Purcella." He was sincerely bad at names!

Dad would struggle to get Riggins' name right for the rest of the visit, and to this day, Tim and I affectionately call him "Regis" from time to time. He will respond to both names.

It was a beautiful, late April day, so we took Dad to Radnor Lake, just south of the city, to walk the paved path at a gentle pace. As we walked, I decided I wanted to try and include him in some of the positive ways he'd participated in my story that he might not be aware of. There was so much we didn't know about each other, so many holes in our shared story, as we only had a handful of encounters in our repertoire.

He'd been tickled, just the day before, when he'd arrived at my time capsule of a mid-century ranch house. I knew he'd graduated from Virginia Tech as an architect in the mid-70's, trying to follow in his own father's footsteps, and I was thrilled that we shared a passion for the same architectural era. I wanted to help connect some dots for him about how he may have been more involved than he knew in me arriving at this house he was so taken with. I wanted him to know we would never have been able to buy our fun, mid-century house had we not first bought and sold our little starter house years before. And that first house wouldn't have been a reality to buy, had Dad not bought me the Acura.

I started to fill him in, wanting to tell him how the insurance money from the Acura had become the majority of our down payment on our first house, so I breached the subject. "Dad, I don't know if you know what happened with the Acura, but" —

Dad interrupted before I could say another word. "Naw! I was in a terrible place back then; we don't need to talk about that!"

I felt a little shut down but persisted. "I want to tell you what a gift it ended up being for us, even after the accident. I want you to know how — through that car — you've provided for me, for both of us," I pointed to Tim who was walking a few steps behind us, documenting our father-daughter outing by sneaking candid photos as we walked together. "You may have played a bigger part than you know, Dad. I do believe everything is made beautiful in time, and I'd love to tell you about it."

He softened, seeming more interested and let me continue. I told him how it had broken my heart to see the car hauled away on the interstate in Columbus on New Year's Eve, but it wasn't lost on me that he had played a part in protecting me that day, and I'd never told him that; I thanked him and told him what the tow mechanic had said about more people walking away from accidents involving an Acura. I also gently mentioned that because we were not in contact at the time of the accident, I'd formed a bit of an unhealthy attachment to the insurance money — money that in my mind, represented his love — and I didn't buy another car for three years. The money had sat in my savings account where I could keep tabs on his affection in dollars and cents, until eventually Tim and I were ready to buy a house and used that money as a down payment. Then, after flipping that starter home, we'd been able to buy the one we were in today that he loved so much.

Dad listened with wonder as I connected the dots for him. I watched his face as I included him in the goodness of my story, it looked like someone was telling him they loved him for the first time. He referenced the hike several times during the rest of the weekend, even mentioning it was his favorite part of the entire trip a few weeks later in a text.

We decided to eat-in that night, Dad was exhausted from our outing, so I offered to keep it simple and make homemade pizza. While the pies were in the oven, I asked him and Tim if they wanted an appetizer of hummus and veggies to munch on while we waited.

"Okay, now what is hummus?" Dad asked excitedly, as if he were about to solve a puzzle. "When I worked at Walmart, people would always ask me where the hummus was. I learned where we sold it in the store so I could point them to it, but I never figured out what it was." He explained his dilemma with innocence and my affection grew for him.

I told him it was mostly chickpeas, olive oil, and salt. I knew from his face that chickpeas left him as dumbfounded as hummus, so I set a bowl of hummus in front of him and said, "See for yourself."

"Scott, can I get you a beer?" Tim asked as Dad enjoyed his first bites of hummus.

"Yeah, okay! I'll take a beer," Dad said with a mouth full of carrots. "Whaddaya got?"

Tim listed off a variety of assortments, "I've got a lager, a Saison, an IPA, or a brown."

Dad looked stuck, like he was hearing a foreign language, before he chuckled his response, "Got any 'just beer?'"

We laughed with him, finally in on the joke that we were a little fancy in our cultured, big-city-life for Dad.

Tim helped him make a selection, asking, "Okay, what do you usually drink?"

"Bud," Dad shrugged, as if there were any other option.

"Great! I think you'll like Yuengling. If you don't like it, I'll get you something else," Tim said as he disappeared down the stairs to his beer fridge in the basement.

It felt good to be together. Dad raved about what a great day it had been; I treasured his delight; it only enhanced my own.

"See, I've struggled with weight since my trucking days—too many cashews and fast food—but I'm motivated by our walk today to get in better shape!" Dad announced after I told him we didn't have any soda to go with his "just beer" and pizza. As I introduced him to sparkling water, he continued, "I used to be really athletic, but after my motorcycle accident, I've had trouble with my leg."

"You have a motorcycle?!" I asked, surprised, but impressed.

"Naw! This was back in high school—you don't know about my motorcycle accident?"

"Dad, let's just assume I don't know anything." I laughed, it felt true, there was so much about this man and his experience on this earth that I didn't know about. But I wanted to know it all. "Will you tell me about it?"

He launched into a story about breaking his leg so severely that he had to be hospitalized for three months. In 1970, they did inpatient physical therapy, so he was stuck in the hospital while he recovered.

"I got sick of doctors and nurses touching me, every day, all the time. For some reason—ever since I was a little kid, I've hated touch. I don't know why; I don't like people touching me—I just recoil from it. Well, I got myself in a little trouble one day in the hospital. I was so fed up being poked, I wedged one of my crutches in the door and moved a locker in front so they couldn't get in." He chuckled at himself bashfully. "Yeah. They weren't too happy with me. Had to get a maintenance guy to take the whole door off."

Listening to him offer his own assessment of not liking touch, I realized his hesitation to hug me was never about me. I wanted to cry as the truth of it penetrated my awareness.

The conversation took a more serious tone, seemingly triggered by Dad's own memory of long hospital stays. "Now, I have decided that I won't be a burden to you, or anyone." He breached the topic with a tone that implied this was not up for debate, and he had given it plenty of thought. "I'm not going to move into a home or stay in some hospital—I don't like doctors, won't even go to one. When it's my time to go, I'll take care of myself." Dad was matter of fact and added, "My brother Steve has your info, you will hear it from him when I'm gone—but only once I'm gone." He made his main point one last time, "I won't be a burden to anyone," before adding, "I'm probably better off dead to you than alive anyway."

"Dad, I hear that you don't want to be a burden, but this also involves me, and I'd like to have a say here. I am the one who decides what is and isn't a burden to me, and in my opinion, I would much rather know you were struggling and be able to care for you in any way possible, rather than have you suffer alone." I could tell he was about to push back, so before he could speak, I went for the one area I knew would soften him, adding, "What about Sarah—who would look after her?"

"Aw, okay, yeah." His jaw lowered, stopping the rebuttal he had been about to deliver. "Now I'm gonna have to think about that." He softened, as the mention of his little dog cracked his armor. For a moment I felt jealous of the dog I'd just used as a pawn to get him to listen to me. She had his heart; he spoke to her with a tenderness and gentleness I'd never received from him, like a father to his young daughter. It stung as I realized this dog received him in a way I never had.

As I accepted that our history was a broken one, an awareness grew within. Although the tenderness I longed for from him wasn't directed at me, I did have an opportunity, here and now, to observe my dad in a gentle, fatherly role. We couldn't go back in time, but it did feel like a gift to be able to experience him this way in the present.

We called it an early night because Tim and I were leading music at church the following morning. Dad was excited to come along, he'd asked if he could come in early with us to listen to us rehearse with the band. He'd been listening to our pastor online and loved his teaching style, so he had $100 in cash ready to give if he "felt inspired."

In the morning, when 6:30 a.m.—our agreed upon departure time— came around, there were no signs of Dad stirring. I checked to see if his truck was still outside, and it was there. *Okay, so he didn't sneak out in the middle of the night.* I was relieved but I couldn't shake the dark feeling I had about his sudden hibernation. Fearing what I may see, I asked Tim to go down to the guest room and check on him. He found the door closed with no sounds of movement or consciousness. The TV was on in the living room, and it appeared Dad had been scrolling through some fire-and-brimstone sermons on YouTube in the wee hours of the morning.

Knocking on Dad's door, Tim asked if he was okay. I heard Dad yell in an almost panicked response, "I'm gonna pass!" Tim asked again if he was okay, and Dad responded through the door that he'd had a rough night and was going to pass on church. Standing at the top of the stairs, I froze. I didn't know what the next right thing to do was. I could feel Dad had withdrawn, and I worried he might leave without saying goodbye, or worse, potentially hurt himself while we were gone. Tim and I could both feel a dramatic shift in the energy in the house, but we decided to give Dad the space he requested, and we left for church.

After the first service, I texted Dad to check on him, and hopefully imply that he hadn't scared us away. He responded with an apology for not coming and seemed embarrassed by the small scene he'd created, regretting he didn't have enough time to make it to the second service. I wanted to continue to invite him in, so I sent him the link to watch online and told him we'd take him to lunch when we were done. He gave me a thumbs up, and I exhaled the tension I'd been holding. At least we had a plan that would keep him from disappearing before I could say goodbye. But once I knew he wasn't a flight risk, tears surfaced for me as I noticed how disappointed I was that he hadn't come.

At lunch, Dad seemed his old talkative self again. I was relieved on one hand, but also felt tossed in the waves of the storm that we'd just weathered. The day before had been so magical, I'd gotten my hopes up that he would enter my world a little further, come meet some of my community, and hear Tim and I sing. But it had proved to be too much for him, so he'd retreated. I was also perplexed by the darkness I could feel that entered overnight. I was lost in thought, working through my disappointment, and hurt.

Dad must've noticed. "Are you okay, you seem different?" he asked bluntly while we waited for our food.

I was impressed that he picked up on it but didn't know how much to share. I was tired, this had been a lot for both of us. I could tell I was dipping into my reserves of grace and generosity, and I would need to recoup once our weekend together was over, but we were still together. He hadn't snuck out in the middle of the night, harmed himself, or left while we were at church, and I was grateful for that much. This visit was still a huge step forward for us and I wanted to try and enjoy our last afternoon together, so I offered the truth with gentleness.

"I'm feeling pretty tired, maybe a little overwhelmed. This was a big weekend for us, Dad. And Timmy and I had an early morning, so I am just taking it all in."

He looked at me for an extra beat before accepting my answer and moving on. I started to bounce back with a little food in my system, and we enjoyed several hours of sweet conversation at Frothy Monkey in The Nations. I could tell Tim and I had earned his trust. Dad listened as we talked about our experience with shame and how crippling it was, tempting us to hide and struggle privately, or put on a facade and emerge as an actor. Tim and I shared some of our own story of descent and transformation with him and explained how we'd found our own path to healing in community and recovery.

At one point, Dad seemed both frustrated and amazed as he exhaled a deep breath and declared, "Golly! Y'all are just so full of grace. You make it look so easy."

He went on to share how he was having some breakthrough in his own life too, but it had come at a price. Almost confessing to me he said, "I've spent over a million dollars of your inheritance to try and earn God's love, and it turns out… He already loved me."

Tim and I laughed knowingly, as we had our own versions of trying to earn God's love, but Dad wanted to make sure I knew he wasn't kidding.

"I mean it, that was money that was supposed to go to you and Matt from your grandmother and great-grandmother, but I kept giving to preachers and ministries, trying to clear my conscience. I am finally realizing that I was loved the whole time."

His awareness felt profound. I'd known my great-grandmother left some money to my dad and his brother that was intended to be passed on, but I also knew they weren't great with their finances, so I had never attached myself to it. I had a lifetime of evidence collected that reminded me I've always had what I needed, from the food stamps that my mom fed us with as children to the money appearing for Tim to go to Onsite. I also wanted my dad to know I wasn't after any money from him, I just wanted to know him, and I loved knowing he was beginning to believe that he had always been loved.

I shrugged my shoulders and smiled at my dad as I said, "I guess it takes what it takes to wake up to what's always been true, Dad."

We went to a movie that afternoon and Dad fell asleep in the theater, snoring loudly during a quiet part of the film. I giggled, looking at Tim with a "what do I do now?" glance, before tapping his arm to wake him up gently, only for him to fall asleep again shortly after. We all went to bed early that night and as we turned in, Dad warned me that he might not be around for coffee in the morning. If he woke up early, he would likely just leave before the sun came up. I was grateful for the warning because when I arose, his truck was gone. He'd snuck out in the wee hours of the morning for Arkansas.

We stayed in touch for the entire year that followed, with simple texts about the dogs, his favorite flavor of sparkling water, and the water kettle he'd bought online during his visit. I even heard my first ever "Happy Birthday" from him, almost exactly a year after his visit. I wrote to him two days later, on his birthday, but I got no response back. That felt familiar, but I checked in a few weeks later as COVID had swept the country that spring. Still no response. I tried a "Happy Father's Day" in June. No response.

It wasn't surprising, this was my dad's pattern. But I didn't have a good feeling about it, this disappearance wasn't sitting well with me. I knew I couldn't make him respond, but because of his fall just before his visit, and learning some of the heart conditions he had, I worried that something might have happened to him, and I would have no way of knowing—especially with my uncle Steve serving as gatekeeper.

Thinking it over, I decided I *did* have other options. Using the serenity prayer, I accepted that I couldn't make Dad respond, but I wondered if someone else might? In June, after not receiving a reply on Father's Day, I looked up Dad's address and found his neighbor. I wrote a handwritten letter addressed to "Dear Current Resident" who lived on the other side of his duplex. I introduced myself as Scott Smith's daughter and explained that I loved my dad very much, but I feared he had too much pride to list me as an emergency contact. I included all my contact info and asked if they would please keep an eye on him for me, as he was getting older, and his health was decreasing.

I knew there was a risk my letter wouldn't be well received or that my dad would find out and be offended that I'd intruded. But I decided I didn't care how the neighbor received it; I wouldn't know if I didn't ask. And I could live with my dad being offended by my attempt to love him and check-in on him, as opposed to sitting passively and letting him disappear again. It was a risk I was willing to take.

To my surprise, I received an email from Tammi the NailGal a few days after I sent the letter.

Hello Stephanie,
My name is Tammi. I received your note in the mail today. I live next door to your father. We've been neighbors now for about four years. He's pretty quiet, but we do say "hi" in the driveway often. He seems to be doing well. I did check on him a week or so ago. I heard a loud bang and was afraid he had fallen. But it was just the wind blowing his door shut. I will gladly keep your information and if anything happens, I'll let you know.

Glad to know he's not completely alone in the world.

Take care,
Tammi

I felt a small amount of relief knowing someone close by was caring enough to keep an eye on him and respond to me, but I felt sad hearing her confirm that he lived shut off from the world around him, so much so, he had been perceived as "alone in the world." He didn't have to be, I wanted to love him. I couldn't control my dad, but I could check on him from afar thanks to a kind neighbor.

What I didn't know then, was that the last I would ever hear from him would be that first happy birthday text he'd sent in April.

Chapter 17
The Phone Call

On Friday, October 16th, 2020, my phone rang with a Virginia number I didn't recognize. Thinking nothing of it, because I was waiting for a tele-health call from urgent care to schedule a rapid COVID test, I answered. As soon as I did, the line dropped, and the call ended. *Ok, back to folding laundry*, I thought as I returned my attention to the show I was entertaining myself with.

Before I could fully re-engage the plot, my phone rang again, but this time, it was a Rogers, Arkansas number. Seeing the familiar city beneath the unknown number, a single thought punctured like an arrow. *This is Dad's neighbor, Tammi, and she's calling to tell me he is dead.* It was more of a knowing than a thought, but it surprised me as it bubbled up to my consciousness. I quickly tried to imagine a different scenario where someone from the same town as my father might coincidentally be calling me.

I answered, and as I intuited, it was Tammi. She introduced herself, reminding me she was Dad's neighbor. She asked if I'd heard from him recently, and I told her I hadn't, he'd gone silent for a few months.

"Well honey," Tammi began cautiously, as if she was still deciding if she was doing the right thing, "I made a promise to you that I would keep an eye on him—damn—I hate to be the one to share this with you, but I did want to let you know that the coroner is at your dad's house right now. He's parked in the driveway, and my husband is over there talking to him. You might want to give the Rogers Police Department a call."

I thanked her, hung up, and immediately looked up the Rogers Police Department. Before I could dial though, the same Virginia number that had dropped minutes before, called again. This time I knew exactly who it was, my Uncle Steve; and he was calling to tell me Dad was dead. I answered, preparing for the syrupy, charismatic veneer I'd encountered 22 years before to greet me on the other end. Sure enough, he didn't disappoint, beginning straight away with pleasantries about how I must be a vision as a grown woman, since I was such a lovely teenager when we'd met at Granny's funeral in 1998.

For nearly five minutes, he proceeded to small talk before finally addressing the reason for his call. "Well, you can probably tell from my tone, it's your dad." For the record, I would have never been able to tell from his glossy delivery that anything was wrong, and my gratitude grew for Tammi's call.

Even if it was only a ninety-second advance notice, I knew at that moment I would forever be grateful that Steve wasn't the one to tell me that my dad was dead. I couldn't control that he had my contact information, which left me feeling vulnerable to a man I didn't know or trust, but the way information had just made its way to me felt like a Holy wink, a reminder that I was held and cared for. I didn't anticipate this to be the path, but as it unfolded, I found myself feeling protected. I didn't let on to Steve that I already knew; with him, the less I said, the better.

Steve told me he just had eye surgery and couldn't travel, but in a generically tender way, he kept saying, "I know you can handle it, Hon. Your Dad said you'd get it taken care of." He then downloaded the landlord's name and number, the coroner's name and direct number, the funeral home, and instructions to cremate, and the detective's name and number, as if he'd had much more time to prepare for this than the rest of us did. He made the biggest fuss about a Trust Officer and spoke as though I should know what he was talking about.

As I intensely wrote down all the information in my journal, the only question I asked was, "Do you know what happened to Dad?"

"Yeah, ah, wey-ell," his southern drawl dramatized as he made 'well' a two-syllable word. "He was in a lot of pain, sweetheart—I mean severe pain. He'd fallen recently and couldn't get around much. He wasn't sleeping and things went downhill from there. He died in his sleep. His heart gave out."

Steve also mentioned that Dad had been struggling for a while and had passed my email, home address, and phone number on to him, but was under strict instructions from Dad to only call once he was gone. I didn't think much of it at the time, it sounded similar enough to the story Dad had told me. Plus, I was in shock as I absorbed this new reality and felt a growing desire to take care of my dad. I got off the phone as quickly as I could, and I jumped into action. This was now my responsibility to take care of.

My first call was to the coroner, who happened to still be at Dad's house. I introduced myself to him as Scott Smith's daughter, and he seemed to have been expecting my call. He'd already spoken with my uncle and knew I'd be getting in touch to run point.

"I'm sorry for your loss Ma'am," he said kindly before continuing to what he assumed I knew. "Yeah, unfortunately, it was a self-inflicted gunshot wound to the head."

Shit! I thought to myself. *Steve, you coward! How could you not tell me it was a suicide?!* I cringed as the awareness dawned that my uncle lived up to every deprecating story I'd heard of him, but unfortunately, as of right now, he was the gatekeeper of some valuable information about my dad that I still needed. As much as I wanted to, I couldn't cut him out yet. I tried to receive the coroner's news gracefully and let him know that my uncle had not mentioned that, and I was hearing it for the first time.

I made several other phone calls, touching base with the funeral home and landlord, before calling Matt and finally Mommy, to deliver the news.

***

Two days later, on Sunday evening, Tim and I made the same eight-hour drive to Rogers, Arkansas, and stayed with our old Nashville neighbors, Gavin and Cait. First thing Monday morning, once the sleepy, southern town emerged from their weekend, I began making phone calls and arrangements. There was so much I didn't know or have access to until we got into Dad's house, but I did have my arsenal of phone numbers from Steve, and I wanted to do everything I could to remove him as the middleman as soon as possible. He was still actively calling the police department, acting as if he was on my team, but I couldn't shake the feeling he was up to something. He had an agenda; I just didn't know what it was. I couldn't bear the thought of him taking advantage of Dad, especially in his death. He'd done it his whole life since childhood. He had played puppeteer, manipulating Dad by his heartstrings. If I had any say in it at all, that was not going to happen with me. My anxiety grew as I sensed my defenses rise, but I wasn't sure what I was defending.

My brother left his wife and daughter in Pennsylvania on Sunday morning and drove 18 hours to meet me in Arkansas, insisting he wouldn't let me face the chaos alone. He arrived Monday night around 9 p.m., and we met at the police department. I'd been getting a runaround all day, as the young lead detective on the case refused to sign the death certificate. I couldn't get Dad cremated without a death certificate, and his body was being stored at the funeral home, charging me a storage fee by the day.

The lead detective had changed his tone on the case throughout the day. Because Dad was unrecognizable when they discovered him, and his ID had been in his truck—not in his home, they needed to send DNA to Little Rock, and it could take up to two weeks. They wanted to make sure it was, in fact, Scott Smith whom they had found. They also wanted to make sure it was a suicide and not a homicide, since they'd found the house unlocked and the back door open. The police kept Dad's wallet captive, with all his credit cards and bank information, as it was considered evidence. I just wanted to settle my dad, there wasn't a question in my mind that it was a suicide, and I hoped that speaking with someone face-to-face might help, especially with my big brother's muscle now giving me courage. Unfortunately, by the time Matt got into town at 9 p.m., the detective we needed to speak with was already at home sipping a beer, so we spoke with a different officer who knew very little about our case. It was clear this was going to be more complicated than expected.

Tuesday morning, our attention shifted to the other mountain set before us: tackling the impossible job of cleaning out Dad's apartment.

The landlord met us at the property and had a dumpster waiting. He'd been kind on the phone when we first spoke on Friday afternoon and advised me to not come until he could hire someone to clean it on Monday. I hadn't even thought of that until he mentioned it, I was just anxious to get to Dad. But as I gave it some thought, it was a suicide, I was grateful to know it would be professionally cleaned and we could focus on settling Dad's belongings and saying goodbye to him.

As I shook hands with the landlord, he warned me it was awful inside and we would want to wear gloves and masks while working because the smell was nothing short of sickening. He gave me a key so we could come and go, then he left us to it. Even with his warning, we were surprised with what awaited us on the other side of the door. I'd been here once before; but what I saw when I entered was almost unrecognizable.

To my shock, Jeff hadn't had the place cleaned, he'd had a good ol' boy down the street come in and rip up the carpet—that's it. The house was a scene from a horror film. All of Dad's belongings were in piles of chaos and disorder around the perimeter of each room. A police officer would later tell me that Dad had sat deceased in his home for at least five days, with a space heater left running directly on him. The house wreaked of a smell so horrific I will never forget it, and words will forever fail to describe it. Dad left a ceramic dinner plate wedged in the back door so his little dog Sarah could get outside—though I don't think she ever left his side; the police had struggled to remove her from the home because she was so defensive of Dad's body when they found him. What Dad hadn't thought through, was that while Sarah would have access to the outside, other things could get inside—and the house was infested with flies.

There was still blood caked on the garage door trim where they had likely struggled to remove Dad's large body through the narrow door frame. Although they had ripped up the carpet in every room, a darkened stain remained on the concrete floor of the room with a "Prayer Room" sign posted on the door. It was obvious a pool of blood had soaked into the concrete foundation beneath where Dad had sat for days.

Matt and I stood in the doorway, looking into that room, and knowing it was the last place our father had been. One of the officers told me there had been a charismatic sermon on repeat blasting through a Bluetooth speaker when they found him. "Seemed like he was tryin' to git right with the Lawrd," the officer offered with an Arkansas drawl. It was the only room that was entirely empty. Nothing but a janitor's bucket and a bottle of bleach remained.

The absence of other things in the room made Matt take notice of a handkerchief thumbtacked to the wall. He entered to examine further as I moved on to another room, surveying the job ahead of us while also grieving the state of Dad's final existence.

It was clear he hadn't been well for a while. There were buckets filled with mirky, discolored water, and bulk packages of pedicure spa tablets and soaking salts where he'd soaked his infected diabetic foot that doctors were threatening to amputate. His medication was chaotically strewn about the kitchen, and cans of food sat half empty and open on his counter, where bugs and mold feasted on the open buffet. Beer bottles were everywhere, and bottle tops decorated the floor as if trashcans didn't exist.

"Don't look behind the scarf on the wall Steph!" Matt yelled sternly, in a way only a protective big brother can.

"Why?" I yelled back curiously now that it was forbidden.

"Just don't. You don't need to see that!" he barked back from the other room.

Dad's small duplex apartment was slightly hoarder-ish from a compulsive online shopping addiction he'd acquired. There were four vacuum cleaners, two of which were still in boxes in the garage. The other two were shop vacs he used around the house, likely to remove piles of filth when it accumulated too much for even Dad to stand. The duplex was flea and rodent infested while spiders and dust filled every nook and cranny. It was clear they were going to have to take this place down to the studs, but first we would have to clean it out.

Where do you start?

I'm so grateful Tim was there. He jumped into action, announcing, "I'll start at the filing cabinet and the desk in the kitchen and look for any important documents. You guys start wherever you want going through his things." He was right, we had one day—two if we were lucky—to get through everything and empty this place, that meant we needed to divide and conquer.

While I began on the boxes in the garage, I watched my brother meet his dad for the second time in his life. Matt went right to his bookshelf and started thumbing through his books and journals, bringing them to me in the garage asking with childlike wonder, "Steph, did you know this? Steph, did he ever talk about this? Who was this person? Steph, did you know?" And in that moment, I realized I had become — even in my limited knowledge and experience of him — the expert on Dad.

Hours into the job of filling the dumpster and sifting through overdrawn bank statements and overdue credit card payments, I walked past the "Prayer Room" again. I glanced in as I breezed by and noticed one of the thumbtacks holding the handkerchief had fallen. It now dangled by a single tack, revealing what had been masked behind it. I stood frozen as I tried to comprehend what I saw. A single bullet hole punctured the wall. A few stands of Dad's thick hair were glued to the circumference of the small hole by a thin perimeter of blood that lined it.

Dad. My heart broke as I talked to him in my head. *I'm so sad.*

I knew he was a high suicide risk. Both of his parents had taken their lives, nine years apart — Lola in 1993, and Jerry in 2002. Dad had struggled and fought for freedom from mental illness, crippling shame, and addiction, but he had struggled in isolation. I thought about him sitting in that room, anguished as he wrestled with the finality of the decision he was trying to make; eventually choosing to pull the trigger. He was 66 years old, and because he had fought most of his battles alone, I knew those years were long and hard. It wasn't bravery in a traditional sense, but I saw the courage it took for him to keep going as long as he had. I was just so sad he hadn't been able to accept any of the help available to him.

He knew I would have come if I had been aware of his condition, that's why he made **Steve** promise not to call me. I felt strangely known and seen by that thought — he was right, I would've been here the moment I knew he needed me. But I also felt angry. Why did he get to choose? Why had I been cut out of this — Dad ghosting me when I checked on him and **Steve** promising him not to tell me how bad it had gotten. Yet here I was — I still came! I just wished I could've come when he was still alive. Why didn't I have a say in this before it ended this way? Why did Steve listen to him? Who agrees to keep a daughter from her hurting and dying father?

***

After fighting another day with the young detective on his first case, it occurred to me that I did know one distinguishing factor about Dad that might help prove it was him without waiting two weeks for DNA results. He had been in a motorcycle accident when he was 16 and doctors put a metal plate in his leg—I didn't know which leg, but thanks to his visit to Nashville the year before, I knew there was a plate!

We met the detective at the station on Wednesday morning before returning to finish at Dad's apartment. Once it was confirmed there was indeed a plate in Dad's leg, he finally released the wallet and signed the death certificate. The detective told us he'd already been in touch with the funeral director and Dad's body was currently being cremated, so we would be able to leave town with his ashes later that afternoon. Thankfully, the funeral home had generously agreed not to charge us for the extra days of storage, and once we finished at Dad's house that morning, Matt and I would be able to pick up Dad's remains and have a few moments together with him before heading out of town. I already knew I would have to make at least one trip back there to get Dad's truck, but it was such a long drive for Matt, I was relieved he was able to leave with some sentiment of closure.

With Dad's ashes acquired and divided between us, and our cars packed with the little bit of his world that we would take with us into our own, Matt asked if we wanted to grab a late lunch before he began his 18-hour drive back to Pennsylvania. I hoped with a presence of Dad with him on his long drive, he would finally get to say some of the things he'd needed to say for a long time to his father.

I still needed to make one final stop at animal control to pick up Sarah before heading out of town, but I was dreading it and grateful to put a lunch in between me and the daunting task.

I can't do it. I can't do it. I thought, finding my limit sitting at lunch and refueling my exhausted body. I hadn't stopped and checked in with myself about the dog, I had just assumed I'd take her because I'd used her as a bargaining chip with Dad. I'd said if he asked me, I would take her. But he hadn't asked. He hadn't left a note. He hadn't said goodbye. He'd blown his brains out and left her, just like he left me. She was terrified, traumatized, and sick from eating God-knows-what while in that house for five days alone. Tim and I had Riggins with us, he'd come along to be the emotional support dog that he is, and I didn't want to traumatize him on the eight-hour drive home either. Even if we all made it home somehow, what was I supposed to do with her? Keep her?

"I don't think I can do it—I can't take the dog." I blurted out, pulling out my phone to call animal control and officially surrender her. Matt was gracious and supportive of my decision, Tim was too, but more so relieved. I put my phone down and decided to wait until after we finished eating to make the call. I just wanted to enjoy a few more moments with my brother before we parted ways.

Shifting conversation, I asked Matt about his wife and sweet little girl, Ava. Casually, I threw out the question, "Do you think you'll have any more kids?" as I stuffed my face with chips and salsa. Mommy had offered her opinion that she didn't think they'd have any more kids, leaving me confident that Tim and I would contribute the next grand baby, regardless of how long it might take us.

Matt's shoulders dropped, and he struggled to finish the bite of food he was chewing. "Well," he said slowly, "I guess I'll just tell you." My stomach dropped; I knew what was coming. This was not what I'd expected when I initiated the question, but I knew before he said it now.

"We're actually pregnant," Matt said with the sheepish grin you'd expect from one revealing a secret. "That's why my wife didn't come with me. I don't want her to travel right now, pregnant in a pandemic—Mom doesn't know yet, so don't say anything!"

I'm not sure what my face revealed, but internally, I felt the bottom fall from beneath me. Up until this moment, I didn't think it was possible to hurt more than I already did. But I was wrong. I'd just found a new depth of grief.

That's not fair! We've been trying for years! How do people have baby's so freaking easily — and for FREE?! My own struggle to conceive flooded my initial thoughts. We were on our fourth IUI with a fertility specialist and the next step would likely by IVF. Verbally, I mustered a pleasantry of congratulations, while inwardly I practiced centering — welcoming a response from a quieter and deeper place within.

More than one thing can be true at the same time. Your hurt and his joy are not mutually exclusive. But now is not the time to ask Matt to hold your sadness. For now, generously hold his joy with him, be with him in his good news — don't demand he be with you in your hurt. This isn't being done to you, it just is what is. Perhaps there will be time for him to hold your sadness later. Until then, trust that there are others who will hold your sadness with you, you're not alone in it.

Finding a more centered place to respond from, and committing to speed dial my therapist on the drive home, I was able to engage in sincere excitement with my brother about the coming addition to our family. Ironically, as Dad had joked in his email to Matt two years before, it would be a baby brother for Ava. In the months to come, Matt would share a piece of Dad with his new son, as he gave him the same middle name as Dad: Hamilton.

We said our goodbyes in the parking lot, and I dialed animal control and told them I couldn't take Sarah, I wanted to surrender her, but I was surprised by the cold response I got.

"You can't do that here; you have to come get her." The woman spoke to me as if I was crazy. "Ma'am. You don't surrender animals here; we are not a shelter. They won't make it."

I had no more fight in me, I was tired beyond words, but I couldn't let Dad's dog be put down. I would have to figure this out later. For now, I was going home with another dog.

We drove across town to the shelter, stopping at Petco to pick up a small dog crate on our way. We could hear her when we got to the office, blood curdling, terrified howls came from the kennel she was in. A volunteer dragged an unrecognizable dog out by a small leash. Her eyes were filled with pus, her coat matted, and she smelled of the now-familiar stench of Dad's house. She wouldn't let anyone close, so they'd been unable to bathe her. She looked like death, she smelled like death, and from the sounds she made the whole eight hours home, it was evident she had witnessed death.

After speaking with the detective who had softened towards me, I began to piece together more of the story—but a few things still weren't adding up. How had Steve known so much when he'd called to tell me Dad was dead? The coroner was still in the driveway, but Steve had the landlord's name and number on standby, and knew his rent was paid up through the end of the month, all within minutes of finding out Dad had passed. How had he already decided on a funeral home to use and provided me with a contact there and instructions to cremate? And lastly, why was he blowing up my phone begging for a death certificate—claiming he wanted to frame it for a small memorial he was going to hold for Dad with his buddies. Who the hell frames a death certificate? He was definitely up to something.

A few days after I returned home, Steve's estranged daughter and my cousin Purcella called to check in on me. Although she'd had a restraining order on her own father at one point, she told me that he was trying to get in touch with her, and she offered to take a call from him if it would help me put together part of the story. I told her I was grateful for any information she could gather, but only to speak with him if she was comfortable. She agreed and took his call the next day. That is how I learned Steve and Dad had planned it all out together. Dad downloaded all pertinent information to Steve, then Steve gave him a few days to follow through on taking his life before calling the cops to do a wellness check. Steve would act surprised when the officers found Dad deceased, then give me all the information I needed to shut everything down because he certainly wouldn't be traveling to Arkansas. Not because he had eye surgery and couldn't drive like he'd told me, but because he was on probation and couldn't legally leave the state of Virginia. *What a guy.*

I was angry learning that my uncle had been an accomplice in Dad's suicide, but I knew the sooner I stopped contact with him the better. He kept nagging me for the death certificate by a certain date, and he was beginning to sound desperate as he continued to make up phony reasons why. I didn't tell him when I finally received the death certificate, but in his urgency to get it, he called the Rogers Police Department and the detective told him he'd already released it to me. Steve demanded I send it to him, his charm dissolving as his true colors appeared. I asked him to disclose why he needed it so urgently and told him I'd be happy to send him a copy once I had settled all of Dad's affairs, but until then, I was running point and unless there was an account I was unaware of, I didn't see why he needed it.

He texted back, "Never mind, I'll handle it myself."

And to this day, that was the last I've heard from him, though he had previously claimed to have gained a second daughter from the tragedy. I don't know what he was after specifically, but I'm sure it had to do with something he stood to gain from Dad's death.

Although I was heartbroken over how my dad had decided to leave this world and that he hadn't let me know how dark it had gotten for him, I was able to accept that he knew how much I loved him, and he was confident I would come if I was aware he was struggling. He didn't want me to know him like that, so he controlled what he could—he kept it from me.

I also knew that I had earned his trust, and he was confident that I would come, once he was gone. I believe he felt safe in the love I had offered him when he was alive, and I wanted to settle him with that same love and care, even as his life ended. I'd spent much of my life pursuing him, refusing to give up on him, and assuring him that I loved him. In the end, and in his own way, it seemed he'd finally believed me.

Chapter 18
Communal Mourning

When Dad passed, a podcast I'd listened to months earlier bubbled up in my memory— David Kessler appearing as a guest on Brené Brown's podcast. Kessler wrote *On Grief and Grieving* with Elizabeth Kübler-Ross, who developed the five stages of grief.

I decided to circle back to it, as it had new relevance for me. I proceeded to borrow Kessler's latest book from the Nashville Public Library and devoured it twice through before ultimately purchasing it for myself.

In the book, Kessler puts a strong emphasis on "Communal Mourning." He writes:

"There seems to be an ever-growing inconclusiveness when the life of a loved one is not marked by an event. We need a sense of community when we are in mourning because we are not meant to be islands of grief. The reality is that we heal as a tribe. There is no greater gift you can give someone in grief than to ask them about their loved one, then truly listen. When we see our sorrow in the eyes of another, we know our grief has meaning. We get a glimpse, maybe for the first time since the loss, that we will survive, and a future is possible."[ix]

It became clear to me that for my own healing, I needed to share my grief with others— grief for both what was, and what wasn't. I'd spent the month after Dad's passing, consumed by settling his affairs, including re-homing his dog Sarah, and driving to and from Arkansas several times. Because he didn't have a community of friends, or any family other than a brother on probation, an ex-wife, and his two estranged children, I hadn't arranged any sort of funeral. As I read Kessler's urging to mourn outwardly and communally, I decided to reach out and invite Mommy and Matt to have an ash spreading ceremony together. However, because of COVID, the approaching holidays, and their own various personal reasons, they both declined my invitation. Although I felt slightly rejected, I accepted their "No" and took ownership of my own need for closure as I brainstormed other options.

I related to Dad so much in his propensity to hide, and his social anxieties since childhood—I too knew the allure of hiding—but he and I had just chosen to deal with it differently. One small decision at a time, played out over the course of a lifetime, had resulted in us living very contrasting lives. His, shut in and alone, privately battling shame and fear of "not getting it right," and mine, rich in a community of trusted ones who knew my struggles, walking beside me, and celebrating my gifts and growth. It occurred to me that this community of people around me, although never having met my dad directly, did, in fact, know him because he was part of me, and I had allowed myself to be known by them.

I asked my church if I could use the sanctuary on Sunday, November 22, 2020, after the morning services, to hold a small memorial for my dad. I wanted to tell a few stories about him, share what I'd learned about him and from him, and honor his life. I wanted to invite people in, and include my dad in the fullness of my community as much as possible; perhaps carrying his story just a little further with the one I was still living.

Coincidentally, November 22 was also my grandpa Ken's birthday, and the sermon that morning was on lament. The day felt strangely inspired. Sometimes, it can be hard for me to sit in my pain, but I have learned that being in it is part of moving through it. I sensed an invitation within the safety of a ceremony intentionally designed to face my grief, in the presence of those who held me when I couldn't bear the weight of holding it all together, to allow both beauty and pain to flood my heart.

I prepared the memorial myself, but had Tim read the welcome so I could get an inventory on how steady I felt once the ceremony started. Tim stood and welcomed our guests, opening with another Kessler passage on communal mourning, to help our friends understand the importance of their presence:

"Funerals and memorials are important. Something profound

happens when others see, hear, and acknowledge our grief. Mourning is the outward expression of our grief. Conversely, something goes wrong when it remains unseen. That's why I believe that when someone decides not to have a funeral, they are missing out. A funeral is the time for people to gather as a family, as a community, to witness grief together. The funeral is the most well-known ritual for death; a ceremony that creates meaning out of our loved ones' experience of life, and our own experience of loss. Saying goodbye is another way we say, 'I love you.'

The funeral ritual is important in witnessing grief because we will grieve alone for the rest of our lives. This is our last formal time to mourn together. One of the most common things we hear at funerals is that our deceased would not want us to grieve for them. I always think: if we can't grieve at a funeral, when can we grieve? The funeral is by design, a communal time to grieve together through music, stories, poems, and prayers. In a memorial, we witness the sadness of the loss, as well as honor the life of the deceased.

People often tell me they're stuck in their loss. I usually ask about their loved ones' memorial or celebration of life. More and more the ones who are stuck in grief say: 'We didn't have one', 'It just wasn't practical', or 'everyone was busy'. Some say, 'We were thinking of doing something in 6 months when everyone could plan, but now too much time has passed' or 'now another family member has died.'

Ceremonies commemorating a loss are not supposed to be practical, easy, or come at a perfect time. When our loved ones die, it is the moment when our grief is most palpable, and witnessing is most needed. There is no completion of grief or closure, but that last ceremony is a book end that acknowledges the final chapter of life has ended. There seems to be an ever-growing inconclusiveness when the life of a loved one is not marked by an event. We need a sense of community when we are in mourning because we are not meant to be islands of grief. The reality is that we heal as a tribe."[x]

Smiling, with his gentle and sincere presence, Tim took his time scanning the room, making eye contact with all forty plus of our friends who had gathered with us. "This is why you are here, friends. Scott's tribe was small, but because he lives on through Stephanie, and his son Matt, his reach is far. He has found his way to you through the life of his daughter. And together, for a few short moments gathered, we share the honor of celebrating the life of Scott and distributing the weight of grieving his death. His life mattered, his gifts mattered, and the world is forever imprinted by his existence here. Thank you for the gift of your presence today. For the generosity of your time and love towards us."

I joined Tim on stage and together, we told many stories about my dad, grieving the complexity of our relationship and the gravity of time spent apart, while also celebrating the time I had with him. We told of his trip to Nashville, just the year before, and the three days spent together. I explained the Little Caesars Hot n' Ready pizzas on a table surrounded by pictures of Dad in the back of the sanctuary, honoring the special homemade dinner we had shared after our walk at Radnor Lake. The memorial spread was complete with veggies and "what-is-hummus," and an ice-cold bucket of "just-beer" to celebrate Dad's simple pleasures with those closest to me.

I shared that my brother Matt had taken Dad's computer home and spent the last month sifting through it. On it, he'd found an architectural floor plan called "Nashville" that had been saved just a month after Dad's visit to me in 2019. In the floor plan, he had created a music studio for me, and a YouTube room for him to make his 'ministry videos,' stemming from a long-time dream of his to be a pastor. He'd designed a master suite for Tim and me on the main floor, and a basement apartment for himself—complete with a video game room.

I framed the floorplan, as it served as a reminder that he was paying attention. Dad was dreaming about a life with me, and he had included my dreams with his. I'd lived so much of my life believing he didn't want to know me, that he didn't think of me, but it just wasn't true.

Matt also discovered that Dad had saved my email on his computer as "Daughter." Perhaps my name to him had always been daughter, and that was one he would never forget. We learned that he only followed seven people on Twitter, and I was one of them. When cleaning out the house, I'd found my contact information scribbled on his desk in multiple places. There were journals with diagrams and sketches with my name on them. One that made several appearances was a triangle, resembling an arrow pointing upward. Written in the bottom left corner was "Scott," with "Steph" in the right, then written at the top where the two corners met to form the point, was "Nashville." Discovering all these hidden gems, it seemed as if God was whispering: *If you ever wondered if he loved you, the answer is YES. You have always been loved.*

My friend, Adam, sang Steffany Gretzinger's, "All That Lives Forever Is Love," a song I still cannot listen to without tearing up, and I closed the memorial with a eulogy I wrote:

Dad,
You were loved the whole time. You've mattered since the day you were born. God wasn't mad at you. You were not a failure. You were never too far gone.

This life, with all its heartaches and complexities, was never meant to be lived or endured alone. The human experience is too heavy to carry outside of relationship with others. The burden of loneliness, shame, guilt, hurt, anger, and fear are all too crushing to bear in isolation. But you tried.

You thought your gift to the world was to become as small as possible, fearing the darkness and brokenness inside might pollute another if you shared it. Not wanting to burden others with it, you closed yourself off and fought your battles quietly and privately.

I know it firsthand to be a risky and vulnerable thing to receive help—especially to ask for help—but I also know it to be the path forward. My greatest sadness is not that you struggled—for to be human is to struggle, you were never alone in that—but that you struggled to believe you were worth helping.

Oh, but Dad, you were! And I believe you know that now. You've come face to face with Love Divine, and you can finally see yourself as fully and freely loved—through the eyes of your Maker, who has always delighted in you.

For years, I have felt protective over you. The more I learned your story, I was able to see you were doing the best you knew how. One cannot give what they don't have, and there was much you were not given yourself. I see the attempts you made to find it; thank you for the efforts you gave, it was brave. You were easily misunderstood, and I wanted to protect you from a world that so quickly judges and criticizes what it doesn't understand. I've found it hard over the past few weeks to release you — still feeling protective over you, even in your passing. But I know I'm not your keeper nor your savior, and I trust the hands you're in now.

So, Dad, I release you.

May you know relationship, love, touch, freedom, and fullness of joy in all its redeemed glory. In your honor, I will continue to pursue a life of fullness and freedom on earth; experiencing the kingdom of God that is here as well as where you are, until we meet again.

I love you.

Your daughter,
Steph

By the end of the ceremony, I knew David Kessler was right. Something had begun to shift in me, and, although I was still sad, I was lighter. I knew the burden had been distributed, I wasn't an island of grief, others had come beside me and offered me the gift of truly listening as I shared. For the first time in months, I had a vision of moving forward. I knew there was more life for me to live, and I felt inspired to include my dad into the fullness of the human experience I was still having.

In the last year of Dad's life, I experienced both more than I ever expected to with him, and so much less than I ever wanted. I continue to live in the tension of those two extremes, careful not to slip into fantasy that it was all reconciled and redeemed in the end, while also deeply grateful for the slivers of redemption we were able to find.

On that beautiful and painful day, I knew I had forgiven him. I had released him from living up to all I had wanted and desired from him. I surrendered my right to resent, retaliate, rage, or revenge. But to assume that is a one-and-done experience only imprisons me from fully feeling in the future. It doesn't allow me to live into new experiences and circumstances that might re-awaken the hurt or longing unfulfilled within me. So, as I stood eating hummus, pizza, and drinking "just beer" after the ceremony with a tribe of safe and strong loved ones who'd gathered around me, I committed to choosing forgiveness again and again — toward my father, my husband, myself, and others. I gave myself permission to have sweet days where I am sincerely at peace and full of gratitude, and to have hard days when it feels as though no one is for me and I've been forgotten once again. Both will inevitably come, and both will pass, but my confidence grew that I could face life on life's terms and somehow hold the paradox that life is tragic, and God is faithful.

Epilogue
Where we are now

From a young age, I deeply desired my father to validate and affirm
my worth and value—from the flesh and bone of my awkward height
to the significance of the soul that resided within it—but he was
unavailable to do so. I carried the question of my significance into the
life I began to create for myself. I hoped a record label could provide
me with an identity, or that success, approval, or validation from
those I deemed important would calm the anxiety within. Later, I
assumed my husband, with his vows to God and me, could redeem
all the broken and rejected pieces of my fractured esteem—proving to
me and the world, once and for all, that I was in fact wanted.

But I kept getting let down. No one could give me what I was looking
for. Perhaps because they were never intended to. Had they not failed
me, would I still be looking for someone else to discover who I am,
hanging my significance on their opinion of me? Would I ever have
begun to look inward and participate with my own feelings and
desires?

The failure of others to provide me with a sense of self-worth or
identity left me longing and searching, until I eventually
discovered that I already had it: it had already been given to me.
Placed there by the Divine when I was knit together and brought
forth into existence.

Love has always been mine. It's always been in me. Yet I spent so
much time and energy outsourcing my worthiness, hoping people,
places, or outcomes could assuage my fear of not mattering. But
belonging was already within me, like a gift I just hadn't unwrapped.
It was mine to open, learn, and use.

Today, instead of assessing my value based on someone else's behavior, I am confident that I am already loved, and worthy of love. Therefore, I try my best to place myself in environments and relationships that are congruent with that and protect myself from ones that are not. Because I am of great value, I will treat myself as such.

Today, I am still married to Tim and couldn't be more excited about it. We continue to learn how to release and return to each other, sharing what we've learned along the way. We practice choosing each other, which means owning when we're wrong and making amends, offering grace when we're wronged, and clearly asking for what we need and want in the relationship.

In the process of writing this book, I climbed the arduous mountain of infertility clinics, navigating four IUI's, two IVF egg retrievals, and eventually one embryo transfer. I intentionally say "I" as opposed to "we" because it was during covid and 1) Tim couldn't even be with me in the doctor's office, and 2) although we were aligned in our shared goal of starting a family, the science experiment was happening in my body, and much of what I found myself lonely and grieving was that my womb wasn't participating in a uniquely womanly experience I deeply wanted to know. It felt like there were certain places Tim couldn't join me in, so I wrote about it. And I am still writing about it.

While the people, places, and things that have failed me most have punctured my heart and given me bruises and scars, they have also provided me with the opportunity to rely more fully on the true Lover of my soul, and for that I am deeply grateful. Could I have discovered these lessons in other ways, without failure, addiction, or mental illness? Potentially. But that's not how my awakening came to me. Therefore, it all belongs somehow. This has been the path that has led me to deep discovery, meaning, and freedom.

I don't believe God delights in our pain, but rather, joins with us in our suffering. I do believe that pain and discomfort have a way of getting our attention, so perhaps God allows it for a time—not causes it—but if nothing slips through God's fingers, then surely all things can be made beautiful in time. Pain will not last forever. All that lives forever is love.

A Benediction

May we find the courage to try again, to reemerge, reconnect, and trust the good that is simply waiting for us to participate with it. Like our brother Adam and sister Eve, stepping out of hiding in the garden, may we respond to love's inquisition of "where are you" by showing up.

May we not be afraid of our desire, but instead use it to engage with our Creator, holding nothing back and inviting the searching of our heart—allowing ourselves to know and be known.

May we receive the moments that pierce our heart as opportunities to collapse in the arms of a God that will never leave us. A God who will join us when our face is in the dirt, and who doesn't force us to get up too soon, but instead invites us to keep going when we are ready, promising this whole thing is headed somewhere good.

May we not fear the death of our expectations, egos, and attachments, but instead find courage from the chartreuse buds of spring that emerge without fail on twiggy, wintered branches, reminding us, new life always comes after death.

May we be willing to let our little kingdoms burn—our need for certainty, comfort, power, and approval—so we might trade the ashes of our best attempts for the beauty and glory of a resurrected life.

May we not be afraid to say, "I'm sorry," and may we continue to seek to grow in understanding, not correctness.

May we not abandon ourselves or fall asleep to our belovedness, for our own heart is the only one we will be accountable for in the end.

May we offer the most generous perspective to others, knowing that we only see a piece of their whole experience, and everyone has their own mountain to climb.

May we be kind to ourselves, remembering we cannot be everything to everyone, and we were never meant to be. It is okay that we are too much for some, and not enough for others, because we are just right for a few.

May we remember that no matter how far down the road we get, we are still ten feet from the ditch, and only humility and honesty will keep us on the path.

May we remember that we did not cause, we cannot cure, and we cannot control another's mental illness, addiction, or recovery, no matter how much we may attempt to, or want to.

And may we know that sometimes it is okay to love from a distance and release others to the care of God.

Let us remember, it takes a lifetime to learn how to live. We've been given one precious life, and all the freedom to decide how to live it. May we wake up to the responsibility that has been given to each of us to participate in this life and remember that our healing often comes when we participate with it. May we not lay on the ground like the man at the pool of Bethesda who became comfortable in his sickness, blaming those around him for his lack of healing. Instead, may we accept the invitation to, "Get up! Pick up your mat and walk." [xi]

1984. Matt feeding me a bottle while Dad listens to records. Tulsa, OK.

1984. Matt, Dad and me. The last time I saw Dad as a baby.

1998. Matt, Dad and me 14 years later.
Standing in Granny's driveway after the funeral.

1984. Our first family photo, Tulsa, OK. Outside our apartment.

1998. Our last family photo, Hammond, LA. Outside Granny's funeral.

February 2019. An 8 Hour Drive for Breakfast—
standing outside the Village Inn.

The Visit. Me soaking up every bit of him, moments after his arrival.
Notice the open wound on his arm, untreated.

The Visit. Dad and I, and his walking stick, at Radnor.

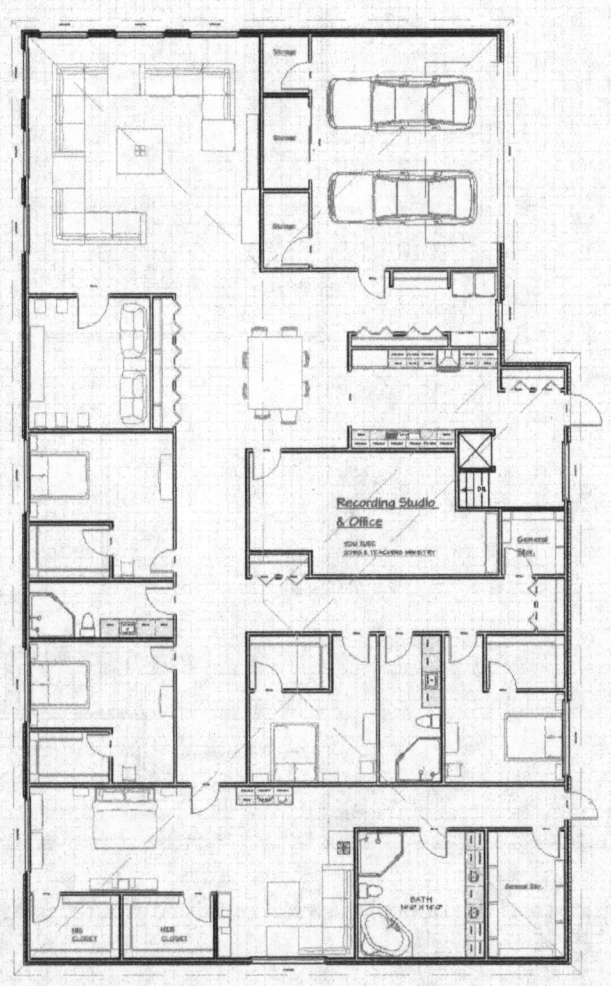

"Nashville_Test" the floorplan saved on his computer in May 2019, a month after his visit to me. He planned a basement apartment with a gaming room for his video game hobby, and a shared office for the "Music & Teaching Ministry" he dreamt of starting with me.

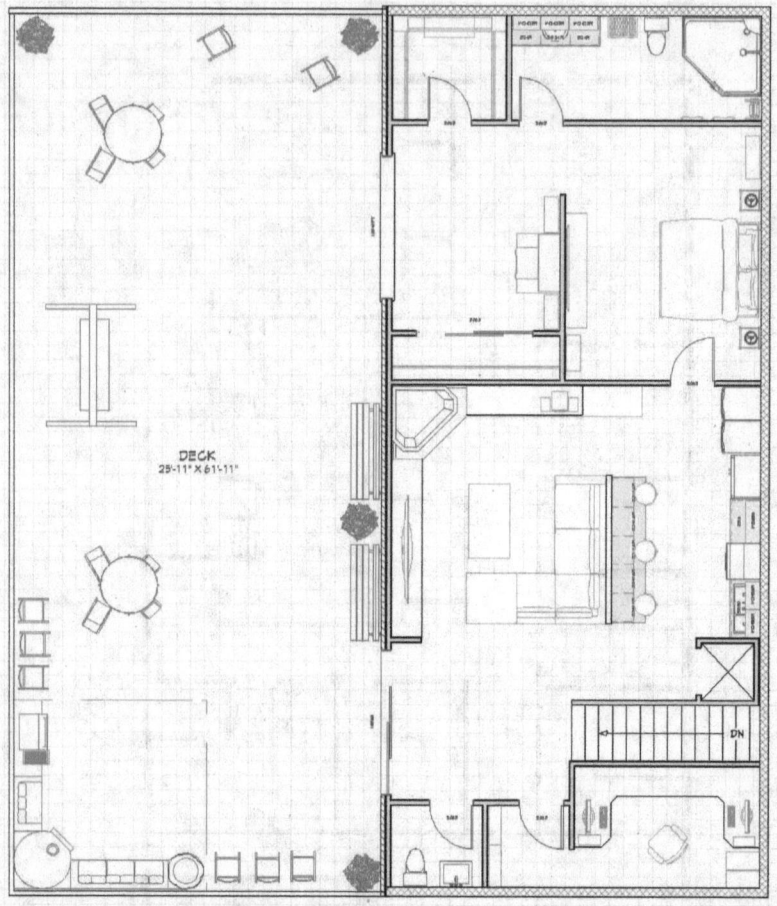

"Nashville_Test" the floorplan saved on his computer in May 2019

Acknowledgements

This might be the scariest part of the book for me because I am terrified to leave someone out. So, let's start here: if I know you, thank you.

Whew, now that that's out of the way. Tim, you generously and bravely allowed me to write some of your precious story because it is impossible to tell mine without yours. You inspire me every day. I want to be more like you in many ways. Thank you for loving me so steadily and for being such a safe place for me to land. I love you Timmy.

Mommy, thank you for allowing me to write a small part of your story as well, I quite literally wouldn't be here without you. Your courage to begin a new life as a single mother of two at 27 will always inspire me. I learned to trust because I watched you trust. I love you.

My big brother Matt, you've always — although you scared all the boys off in High School — looked out for me, even when it meant driving 18 hours to join me in settling Dad.

Dad, thank you for teaching me so much without realizing it. It is my joy to share our story with the world, you have always been worth knowing.

Rob Bell, you helped me untangle the hairball this story was initially and with your wizard-like questions, you assisted me in finding the order I somehow always knew it existed in.

Caitlin Elizabeth, thank you for being my word-baby doula. Your gentle and nurturing assistance in editing and bringing this final draft across the finish line came at the perfect time. You are a gift.

Brent French and Rachel Rondell, thank you for your skill, expertise and patience with me in bringing this cover design to life.

Carol Jones, thank you for the first round of edits that helped me get it all on the page.

From here we will rapid-fire in no particular order, buckle up... Renee & Matt Olson, Cait & Andy Butcher, J & Sara Hall + Eli, Xander, & Liam Hall, Lindsey Davis, Emily Scott, Adam Agin, Lindsey & Jonathan Frazier, Anais & Joey Ramirez, Claire Tyner White, Jonathon & Suzy Weibel, Anya Dvirnak Lydia & Don Hejny, Doug Sabel, Suzie Lind, Mike Erre, Kevin Dixon, Tim Timmons, Betsy Raney, Tessa Violet, Courtney Shaddox, Ashley White, Katelyn & John Hill, Bob & Dannah Gresh, Lexi Gresh, Don Pape, Julian Vaca, Brock & Auny Gill, Angelica Smith, Todd St John, Brian Holliday, Kelly & Stephen Horvath, Jeff & Sue Bogan, Tim & Cathy Johnson, Dave & Leah Bell, Kathy & Ron Bartoo + Seth, Rachael & Cherie Marie, Donna Waldhausen, Tristan & Miriam Lobb, Trewyn Lobb, Tessa Mosley, Karl Hosterman + Brandon, Daniel & Kevin Hosterman, Diane Hosterman + Josh & Kristina Daly, Kent & Ruby Skipper, Kristin & Tim Donnell + Malia, Koen, Lincoln, Sarah Smith + Ava & Calvin, Lara Parks, Leslie Jordan, Toby McKeehan, Joey Elwood, Kyle & Kristy Chowning + ROOTS Academy, Erica Manthey, Ashley Siner, Jennifer Lewis, Jody Johnson Hill, Sharry Kitchell, Alli Worthington, Grant & Penny Harrison, Colin & Michelle Rigsby, Lizzy M, Vicky M, Gina S, Gina F, Shelby 615, Shelby 703, Jill G, Al Andrews, Eli Machin, Ethan Luck, and 8th & Roast for all the discounted coffee in the process of writing this book.

About The Author

Photo credit: Kylie Sivley

Although many have tried—and may even believe they have accomplished similar—Stephanie has succeeded in finding the most amazing dog in the whole world and her favorite thing to do is be with her pitbull, Riggins. She lives in Nashville, TN and sings in an 80's & 90's cover band called Rubiks Groove around town on weekends. She teaches voice lessons part time and enjoys assisting others in finding their voice—metaphorically and literally. She manages two Airbnb properties and loves hosting karaoke parties in her 70's basement. Quirky, strange, and unique things still catch her eye, and today she has an entire closet dedicated to her thrift store coats. In addition to her hobby of renovating houses, her latest interest is car restoration, and she can be spotted on a sunny day, driving her baby blue 1989 BMW 325i convertible named "Birdie," with Riggins riding shotgun.

Citations

i Rohr, Richard. "Ego: The Actor." *Center for Action and Contemplation*, 5 July 2016, https://cac.org/ego-the-actor-2016-07-12/.

ii De Mello, Anthony. *The Way to Love: Meditations for Life*. Image, 2012.

iii De Mello, Anthony. *The Way to Love: Meditations for Life*, Image, New York, 2012, p. 36.

iv *Working the S-Anon Program*, S-Anon International Family Groups, Nashville, TN, 2003, p. 125.

v *Peter Crone: The mind architect on what our feelings are trying to tell us*. Listen Notes. (2020, June 11). Retrieved July 6, 2022, from https://www.listennotes.com/podcasts/enough-is-enough/peter-crone-the-mind-Nbvt0c6aC-o/

vi *Twelve Steps and Twelve Traditions*, Alcoholics Anonymous World Services, Inc., New York, NY, 2020, p. 53.

vii Singer, Michael A. *The Untethered Soul*. New Harbinger Publications, 2020.

viii Young, William Paul. "Is Transformation Possible without Pain?" *Wm. Paul Young*, 21 July 2015, https://wmpaulyoung.com/is-transformation-possible-without-pain/.

ix Kessler, David. *Finding Meaning: The Sixth Stage of Grief*. Scribner, 2020.

x Kessler, David. *Finding Meaning: The Sixth Stage of Grief*. Scribner, 2020.

xi John 5:8